Universal Grammar of Story™
The Workbook

Hazel Denhart Ed.D.

Universal Grammar of Story™: *The Workbook*
© 2020 Hazel Denhart, published by The Invisible Press, Seattle

Library of Congress Control Number: 2019913194
Denhart, Hazel
Creative writing—Fiction: authorship, study and teaching, theories of, how-to, methodology, philosophy of, mythology in; hero's journey; workbook
Literary Nonfiction: authorship, study and teaching, theories of, how-to, methodology
Creative writing guides
Literary theory
First edition
Pages 124
Includes bibliographical references

ISBN 978-1-936262-04-5 (workbook paperback)
1. Creative Writing. 2. Fiction—authorship
PN3355-3383 Technique. Authorship
Annotation: *Universal Grammar of Story*™: *The Workbook* is the companion study guide for the main text: *The Universal Grammar of Story*™: *An Author's Guide to Writing for the Soul of the World*. This workbook provides practical support for story writing with worksheets, templates, study questions, individual exercises, advanced exercises, and direction for conducting literary salons. Suitable for textbook adoption.

Keywords: creative writing workbook; literary nonfiction guide; writing technique workbook; study guide; writing salon; storytelling workbook; stories; mythopoetic instruction; call to write; writing worksheets, playwriting workbook; screenwriting workbook; mythology workbook; story structure workbook.

All Rights Reserved. No part of this book may be reproduced in any form or by any electronic or mechanical means, including information storage and retrieval systems without permission in writing from the author, except by reviewers, who may quote brief passages in a review.

Inquiries should be addressed to:
The Invisible Press, 7001 Seaview Ave NW, Ste. 160-474, Seattle, WA 98117
info@invisiblepress.com, phone: 206.282.8211, fax: 212.202.6329

Artist Acknowledgments appear on 115.

universalgrammar@invisiblepress.com
www.hazeldenhart.com

1 2 3 4 5 6 7 8 9 10 PM 20

DEDICATION

For You, the Writer.
Yes, you really are a writer.

CONTENTS

PREFACE viii
INTRODUCTION x
Prerequisite Exercises xii
Chapter One: The Personal Call 1
   Individual Exercises 2
   Literary Salon 6
Chapter Two: The Social Call 9
   Individual Exercises 10
   Literary Salon 12
Chapter Three: The Mythological Call 15
   Individual Exercises 16
   Literary Salon 16
Chapter Four: Thinking in Balance 19
   Individual Exercises 20
   Literary Salon 24
Chapter Five: Awakening to Language 27
   Individual Exercises 28
   Advanced Work 29
   Literary Salon 30
Chapter Six: Delilah's Scissors 33
   Individual Exercises 34
   Advanced work 35
   Literary Salon 36
Chapter Seven: The Plot Situation 39
   Individual Exercises 39
   Advanced Work 42
   Literary Salon 44
Chapter Eight: Opposition and Conflict 47
   Individual Exercises 47
   Advanced Work 49
   Literary Salon 51
Chapter Nine: Story Chemistry 53
   Individual Exercises 53
   Advanced Work 58
   Literary Salon 59
Chapter Ten: The Structure of Timing 61

    Individual Exercises..61
    Literary Salon..66
Chapter Eleven: Joseph Campbell's Hero's Journey...................69
    Individual Exercises..69
    Advanced Work..72
    Literary Salon..73
Chapter Twelve: A Moment in Heaven with Aldous Huxley 75
    Individual Exercises..75
    Literary Salon..77
EXAMPLE ANSWERS 79
    Prerequisites Exercises 81
    Chapter Two 101
    Chapter Four...103
    Chapter Eight..104
    Chapter Nine 108
    Chapter Ten 110
    Chapter Eleven.. 112
REFERENCES.. 114
ART SERIES ABSTRACTIONS 115

WORKSHEETS

Worksheet 1: Character Relationships 5
Worksheet 2: Generational Primal Archetypes for
the Study Story 10
Worksheet 3: Generational Primal Archetypes for
Developing Story 11
Worksheet 4: Syllogistic Reasoning 21
Worksheet 5: Outer Body Experiences 21
Worksheet 6: Inner Body Experiences 22
Worksheet 7: Face Facts 22
Worksheet 8: Core Reactions 23
Worksheet 9: Emotional Reactions 23
Worksheet 10: The 36 Dramatic Situations for
Study Story and Others 39
Worksheet 11: The 36 Dramatic Situations for
Emerging Story 41
Worksheet 12: The 36 Dramatic Situations for Subplots and
Minor Characters 43
Worksheet 13: Hero-Villain Polarity 48
Worksheet 14: Incremental Polar Movement 49
Worksheet 15: Events Triggering Polar Movement 50
Worksheet 16: Collective Forces Triggering
Hero's Transformation 50
Worksheet 17: The Five Elements for Study Story 53
Worksheet 18: Five Elements of the Hero's Proposition for
Your Story 55
Worksheet 19: State of Affairs for Study Story 56
Worksheet 20: State of Affairs for Developing Story 56
Worksheet 21: Full Proposition with prompts for
Study Story 57
Worksheet 22: State of Affairs for Developing Story 57
Worksheet 23: State of Affairs for the Antihero of
Developing Story 58
Worksheet 24: Timing Milestones for Study Story 61
Worksheet 25: Concept of Emerging Story Timing 63
Worksheet 26: Hero's Journey for Study Story 71
Worksheet 27: Hero's Journey for Emerging Story 72

TABLES

Table 1: Structure of the Logical Syllogism 20
Table 2: Example of Unsound Major Premise 20
Table 3: Example of Minor Premise not Following the Major....20
Table 4: Universal Grammar of Story™ Interpretation
of Huxley 75
Table 5: Huxley's Original Themes...76
Table 6: The Seven Deadly Sins..77
Table 7: Genres and Meanings 81
Table 8: Character Types..83
Table 9: Archetypal Family Roles 86
Table 10: Social Functions for Characters................................87
Table 11: Professions for Characters...89
Table 12: Character Dispositions..93
Table 13: Example of Generational Primal Archetypes for
The Miracle Worker 101
Table 14: Example of Bad Logical Reasoning 103
Table 15: Example of Corrected Logical Reasoning 103
Table 16: Examples of Unity of Opposite Pairs 104
Table 17: Hero Villain Polarity Example................................. 106
Table 18: Example of Incremental Polar Movement................ 107
Table 19: Example of The Five Elements of
the Hero's Proposition for *The Miracle Worker* 108
Table 20: State of Affairs for *The Miracle Worker* 109
Table 21: Timing Milestones for *The Miracle Worker* 110
Table 22: Hero's Journey for Helen in *The Miracle Worker* 112

FIGURES

Figure 1: Universal Grammar of Story™ Chart of Theories 78
Figure 2: Mind Map for *The Miracle Worker* 97
Figure 3: Mind Map for *Bite Your Tongue* 98
Figure 4: Positive/Negative Character Relationships for
Bite Your Tongue 99

PREFACE

The Universal Grammar of Story™ is a rich intellectual inheritance coming to you from your literary ancestors of long ago. Your role is to grasp their teachings, put them to use in the service of humanity, and pass the wisdom along to the coming generations through stories.

"The Grammar" is a vibrant, dense, and multifaceted body of knowledge meant to arrive slowly and unfold in accordance with its own destiny. This graceful body of work might take decades to find its way into the wider writing community. That you have the workbook in your hands now is a subtle sign that you were intended to be one of the early recipients.

INTRODUCTION

This workbook is a companion study guide for the main text of *The Universal Grammar of Story*™: *An Author's Guide to Writing for the Soul of the World*. The workbook provides practical tools for navigating deeper into the multiple levels of the original text, making it easier to learn and apply the theories of The Grammar to any story. The exercises range in complexity from easy to quite challenging.

It's best to approach them intuitively, working with those that feel just difficult enough and waiting on the more advanced challenges for the future. But don't let yourself off too easily. Remember from the main text that struggle is important for advancing your development.

This workbook is intended as a practical guide to apply to stories. It can be used anytime in the writing: before, during, or even after a story is written. You can use it:

- ❖ Before a single word hits the page;
- ❖ After some writing has been done but the story seems to stop;
- ❖ After hundreds of pages are written but the story just seems to go in circles;
- ❖ Returning to a story you gave up on years ago, but which will not give up on you;
- ❖ To bust out of any form of writer's block;
- ❖ To analyze what makes a well-loved story particularly strong;
- ❖ To find out why a box office flop flopped; or
- ❖ To help your friends figure out why their stories are stuck in writer's block.

The chapters of the workbook follow the same order as those of the main text of *The Universal Grammar of Story*™: *An Author's Guide to Writing for the Soul of the World*. However, a "prerequisites" chapter has been added for writers who have only a vague idea for a story and need to develop a more concrete grasp of it before putting it through the paces of the chapters to come.

Many aspects of The Universal Grammar of Story™ can be easily grasped and immediately put to use. But there are other deeper dimensions that develop slowly with dedicated practice.

This body of wisdom is one we never outgrow. It evolves with us becoming ever more multifaceted as our focus shifts with maturity and life experience. Younger writers tend to be more interested in the nuts and bolts structure of writing found in the chapters on the core theories. Older writers, even those just taking up their first story, tend to be more interested in the fundamental philosophies of the Call to Write and the mystical ones weaving together the chapters on mythology. Regardless of where you might fall on the career path, there is a seat of wisdom waiting for you in the one-room schoolhouse that serves as this book. For aspiring writers (including those who have yet to set a word to paper) it introduces the fundamentals of why we write and for whom, as well as how to get those words to stick to the paper and behave themselves. For the advanced career writer, it reveals why those unwelcomed moments arrive when the story stubbornly goes on strike for no apparent reason. Understanding The Grammar makes such moments more predictable but they will never be preventable. Like the tide rising and falling, the ebb and flow of writing is a vital and inevitable part of the rhythm of life.

OK, here we go…

The Blessings of Trouble

Sometimes writer's block comes after months of feverish work and sometimes it happens before a single word finds its way onto the first blank page. Regardless of the timing, sooner or later most every writer experiences the distress of enthusiasm fading as a streak of creativity runs its natural course and the story grinds to a customary, inevitable, and agonizing stop. It's a lot like parenting. The newborn comes with a bounty of excitement, aspirations, and hope; but eventually the child turns into an adolescent and nothing seems to go according to plan. You find yourself at wits end and exhausted in the face of unrequited love for a being who is the center of your universe.

Not to worry. When the creative flow slows it will be time for this workbook. Until then its best to let your creativity run amuck with unfettered intuition in a mind where things are still spontaneous, giddy, and not yet over-thought.

You will need to bring two stories to this workbook. The first will be the one you are writing that's playing hard to get. It doesn't matter whether it still only exists in your thoughts as a vague idea or if you have already written 500 pages. You will also need a second, "study story." This needs to be a well-known favorite that you are not likely to tire of. Beloved stories act like favorite hymns, recitations, or chants—so comforting they never grow stale.

Writing salons using this workbook for group study will also need to choose one study story for the entire group that is different from those of the individual members.

Films are ideal for working through the lessons providing you have the technology to pause, fast-forward, and rewind segments in order to pinpoint moments that align to a given point. Film and play scripts also work well; however, any form of story is suitable (novel, epic poem, short story, etc.) provided it is well-known and loved.

For the writer whose emerging story is still a vague idea that cannot quite be grasped, the exercises and worksheets below will help you develop it enough to carry on through the coming chapters.

Prerequisite Exercises

Try not to overthink your answers. It is best to let your intuitive mind work free and unrestrained which happens by choosing what grabs you first. There are no right or wrong answers. This is a simple play of serendipity. You will find charts and sample answers to guide you in the Prerequisites' Example Answers at the end of the book.

1. Identify the type of work (novel, film, etc.) and give a working title for your story.
2. Is the story a comedy or tragedy? If it is a mix of both make a binary decision as to whether it tends to be more serious or funny.
3. Choose your genre and explain your choice. See the Example Answers on page 81 for a chart of genres and their meanings. Some stories might be a blend of more than one, but one will take the dominate role. For example, *Hamlet* is both a tragedy and a family drama, but it is classified as a tragedy.
4. Generate a list of character types describing your protagonist. Is this person a commander? A wise elder? An evil lord? A

gentle giant? An eccentric pixie girl? Or a blend of more than one? See the Example Answers on page 83 for a chart of character types.

5. What *symbolic* extended family/tribal role does the main character fill? Think of your characters as if they were in an ancient tribal world. In purely symbolic terms, cast your protagonist into an energy type that we understand on a familial level. Does the protagonist project the energy of a father, stepmother, daughter, cousin, aunt or half-brother, etc.? A character need not appear as an actual step-uncle in the story to project that kind of energy. See the Example Answers Table 9, page 86 for a chart of symbolic family roles.

6. What is the protagonist's name and meaning? Names are powerful things and must reflect the personality of the named. Turn to a book of baby names or baby name website to search for names based on character type, or to learn the meaning of a name you have already chosen. Obituaries also provide a good source of names.

7. What is the protagonist's social function within the community/tribe? Communities naturally bring together diverse individuals whose given functions provide benefits or detriments to the group. Even a seemingly homogenous group will still yield a: peacemaker, complainer, gatekeeper, monopolizer, etc. A single character might well take on more than one function. See the Example Answers on Table 10, page 87 for a chart of social functions.

8. Choose a profession for your main character and imagine how the character came into this career. See the Example Answers on Table 11, page 89 for a table of nearly 300 professions.

9. What is your protagonist's disposition? Is your character generous? Stingy? Kind? Cruel? Several types may apply to the same character. See the Example Answers on Table 12, page 93 for an example of potential dispositions.

10. Sparking the beginning of a natural conflict is straightforward once you identify the protagonist's character type and disposition. All you need do is:
    A. Choose the antonym of the character type you chose (#4 above).

B. Choose the antonym of the character disposition you chose (#9).
C. These words represent the opposing force the protagonist will encounter in the story. Form a sentence of these words that will develop into the heart of the conflict that the story exists to resolve. See #10C on page 96 for an example.

11. Brief summary of the story.
    A. Gather your answers from questions 1-10 in a simple list.
    B. Use the list to write a brief summary of the story. A simple paragraph is enough but if the spirit moves you write until you feel like stopping. See #11B on page 96 for an example.

This chapter has guided you in materializing the main character of your story. Later on, as the story grows more confident in your mind, repeat these exercises for the supporting characters.

Chapter One
The Personal Call

The personal call to write urges us to tackle unresolved problems disguised as characters we project into stories. It acts a bit like the butterfly's cocoon—the place where a story sparks to life and germinates but which also must be overcome and cast away before its structure turns oppressive and kills the very thing it came to give life to.

In this chapter we explore what might be calling us to a given story. Luckily, the gift of writer's block helps us with this puzzle. When it hits for no apparent reason and the infatuation fades into hard work, it's time for this chapter. What feels like unrequited love is in fact a valuable and necessary moment that can be enormously helpful in penetrating an elusive story.

One of two things is likely to happen when a writer's block is taken down by means of the personal call: Either the story will burst forth and return to writing itself, or it will utterly collapse and appear to die. When the latter happens, we have likely mistaken the story for what was merely a momentary means of dealing with a personal issue. In this case, once you resolve the issue, the story will have served its purpose and disappear. This doesn't mean that the work is a total loss. Not at all. It means it has served its purpose for now. If so, this would be the time to respectfully set the manuscript into a pretty box in the attic. It might just need time (perhaps even twenty or thirty years) to germinate into something else. What you have written could be the premonition of a radically different story awaiting you in the future. Or, it could be that this is not a story of its own but a piece belonging to another story. So, hold onto it.

With that in mind, when you address the personal call bear in mind it:

- ❖ Should not be "work" and should never be forced.
- ❖ Sends images into our daydreams from the unconscious.
- ❖ Triggers stories to tackle personal problems from the safe distance of fiction.

❖ Can be identified by a metaphor appearing in a single sentence summary of the story.
❖ Can be identified by the relationships between other characters in the story.

A note of caution: few writers are aware of the personal call which by its very name is a private process and not something to openly share without careful forethought. Also, exercises like this can be exciting for some while unpleasant for others. Remember, it is not necessary to do these exercises to write a great story. They simply offer a tool to better understand your relationship to the symbols that characters might represent to you. The following exercises guide you in exploring your story as a metaphor for your life, or perhaps as a message from you to your own self.

Chapter One: Individual Exercises

Story Description Exercises

Answer the questions below for your study story. Then repeat them for the one you are writing. See the answer key in Example Answers beginning on page 97.

1. Make a mind map for your study story. Write the title of the story at the top of a blank sheet of paper. In the center of the page write the first word that comes to mind about it. Draw a star-shape around this word. Next, in random places on the paper, jot down about a dozen or so stream of consciousness words in rapid-fire succession. Circle each word as you write then draw a connecting line to the word in the star or another on the page. The words might all connect back to the center or not. Perform this exercise by intuition, by feel. Try not to think logically about it.
2. Compose a sentence from the words you have generated above. Add additional words as necessary. Avoid specifics; keep it general.
3. Refine the sentence into a simple description of the story. Keep it generic enough to apply to any story, anywhere, at any time in history.
4. Contemplate how the description might have attracted you to this story.

5. Repeat 1-4 for the story you are writing.

Character Relationship Exercises

The following exercises are intended for the story you are writing, but they can also be applied to the study story to expand your understanding of character dynamics. They explore the connection between characters, as well as between the writer and characters. In the center of a blank piece of paper, draw a sun symbol large enough to write a character's name in its center. See worksheet 1, page 5.

6. With a clock face in mind, quickly write the names of all your characters on the periphery where the hours would be. If you haven't settled on names yet, then jot down the roles characters might play. This should be done in brainstorming fashion without analysis or thoughtful recall. The idea is to get outside of your logical mind.
    A. Circle the names and draw a straight line back to the sun center. If you have only a few characters, the image will resemble a pie with large pieces. If you have several, it will look like a clock or even a bicycle wheel with spokes leading to the hub.
    B. Make as many copies of this image as you have characters, plus one additional.
    C. On the first copy, write the protagonist's name in the sun center. Then indicate that character's feeling toward the others by marking the connecting line with a negative (-) or positive (+) symbol. The line connecting the same character at the center and periphery indicates that character's sense of self.
    D. Repeat the above with the additional sheets so that each character has a sheet of their own. In this way, the feelings of all the characters toward one another is better understood.
    E. On the remaining sheet, write your name in the sun center and indicate your relationship to the characters.
7. On a blank sheet of paper, write the word "To" at the center top. On the left side below, list all the characters followed by the word "Represents" after each one. Make as many copies of the page as you have characters plus one additional.

A. On the first sheet, write the protagonist's name at the top and indicate below what each character represents to this person.
B. Repeat with the other sheets for each of the other characters. On the line where a character's name appears on both the top and below, indicate the sense of self. Note that the relationship will not necessarily be the same both ways. What Hamlet means to King Claudius is very different from what Claudius means to Hamlet.
C. On the remaining sheet, write "Me" at the top center and list what each character represents to you.
D. When you are finished, pencil in who you think each character could represent from your past or present life, real or imagined. A character might also represent a future version of yourself that you envision, or someone else you hope will come in the future.
E. Contemplate the underlying metaphor or reason these characters have appeared to you in the daydream of your story. What message might you be sending to yourself? In other words, if your story were a dream, how might it be interpreted? What is the over-arching metaphor?

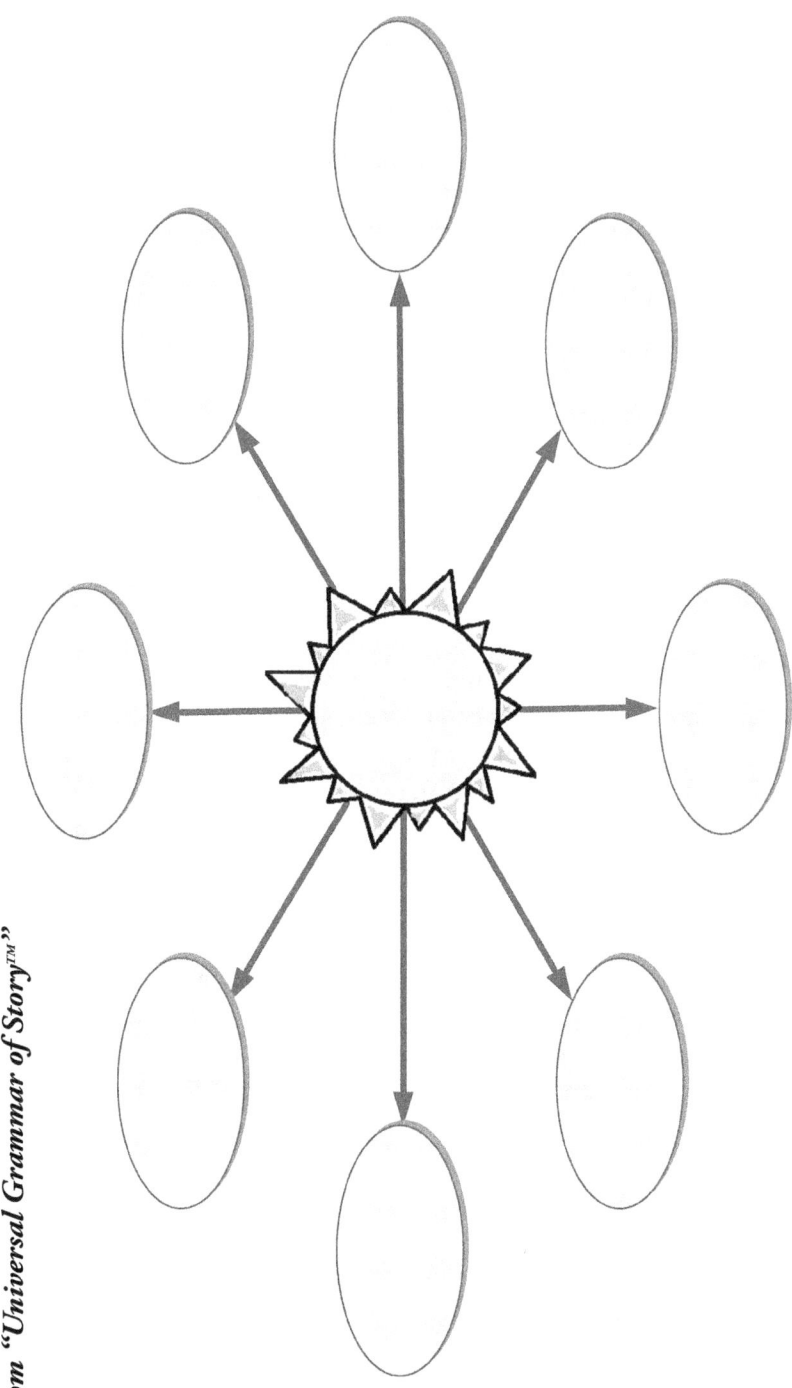

Worksheet 1: Character Relationships
From "Universal Grammar of Story™"

Chapter One: Literary Salon

Forming the Salon

1. Begin forming a salon by bringing together a group of no less than three but no more than ten people. Six is ideal. If eleven show up, form separate groups which still come together as a whole for staged readings and other social activities.
2. Consider including other narrative artists such as musicians, photographers, and painters, etc.
3. Be mindful of group chemistry by seeking a diversity of members while avoiding close friends and relatives. Members need fresh insight from those who are less likely to prejudge their ideas based on history with each other.
4. Find a meeting place with a literary or creative intellectual feel such as a bookstore or literary café, public library, college campus or school, or community center, etc. Try to avoid online meetings if possible because digitally mediated conversation does not hold the same synergy as good old-fashioned vis-à-vis encounter.
5. Create an inviting atmosphere with some gentle classical music played low, a plant, center piece, and/or warm lighting.
6. Think of the salon as a think tank where your mind and action need to be at their best (like the 9 a.m. meeting in Geneva to save the world—even though you are meeting in the evening). Keep the meeting time to about two hours with a frequency of no more than twice a month. Once a month is a good rule at first.
7. If the group is comfortable with it, you might consider having a staged reading, publishing a zine, or exhibiting members' work once a year.

Agenda for the First Meeting

1. Keep the atmosphere playful by coming together for a meal if possible. The purpose of this first meeting is to establish the group, get to know one another, agree on a permanent space and share summaries of members' work in progress.

2. Choose a core study story to analyze together over the next several months. Consider beginning with a film that salon members can easily watch together.
3. Each salon member still needs to choose a separate story for personal study.

Agenda for Following Meeting:

1. Discuss Chapter One of the main text *The Universal Grammar of Story™: An Author's Guide to Writing for the Soul of the World.* How relevant is this chapter to the experience of the salon members?
2. Watch the first 25 minutes of the group study film together. You should feel a natural break in the story about that time.
3. What metaphors do group members see in the core study-story? Is there unanimous agreement on the metaphors? If not, do some members see a different tale than others?
4. What life story can the salon members extrapolate for the writer of the study-story? In other words, in viewing the story as a dream of the writer, what do you imagine the life of that writer to be like?
5. What life events or themes in the writer's personal life might have triggered a conscious or unconscious need to generate this tale?

NOTES:

Chapter Two
The Social Call

Chapter two expands our investigation of the call to write into the social sphere where writers' personal needs give way to that of the collective. Here, writers move beyond the self, in service to something greater: society's struggle against the crushing threat of atrophy brought on by the status quo. The world begs its writers to "do something!" Yet more often than not it paradoxically refuses to cooperate or even recognize the writer's vital work. Even so, in such lonely moments, writers persevere and through their characters push the wheel that keeps our social world evolving.

While the personal call changes over the course of a writer's life as problems come and go, the social call by contrast remains ever the same throughout its era. It also remains the same across all creative disciplines: Painters, poets, composers, writers, and performing artists of all walks are drawn together by the force of a single, grand collective need. In Modernity that need was to restore our humanity against the heartless brutality of the industrial world. The echo of that summons can still be heard although it is fast fading. As postmodernity takes its dominant role, we are ever more strongly called to guide society to tribal reunion in the aftermath of modernity's brutal scattering us from one another.

The exercises below direct you in recognizing the social call. They also direct you in analyzing rudimentary character archetypes based on the work of Carl Jung. A balance of archetypes is necessary for a cohesive tribe to emerge and hold together throughout the story. While hundreds of archetypal roles exist, here we just need those primal, symbolic family roles projected by characters. Such include father, mother, child, grandparents, etc. On a metaphorical level these roles are not concerned with age. For example, a child might carry out the role of a parent figure as in Ben Zeitlin's film, *Beasts of the Southern Wild*. Here, we see the mother figure develop in a six-year old girl named Hush Puppy. Likewise, in stories about men at sea, one will take on the mother role, another the grandmother role, etc. (although it is possible for one character to symbolize more than one role).

For the purpose of these exercises, the terms "hero" and "villain" refer to Jungian concepts of these archetypes—primal symbols of good and bad—not to be confused with the actual hero and villain/antihero of the Universal Grammar of Story™ proper, taken up in the core narrative theories to come.

Chapter Two: Individual Exercises
See Example Answers on page 101.

1. Is your chosen study-story aimed at modernity or postmodernity? Specify the elements that represent this and explain what changes would be needed for an audience of the other era.
2. How might you answer the postmodern craving for re-tribeing or reconnection in the story you are writing?
3. Distribute the characters of your study story among the generational primal archetypes using the worksheet below. (Remember, the generational role a character plays need not fit the actual age of the character).

Worksheet 2: Generational Primal Archetypes for the Study Story

Story Title:		Author:
Archetype	**Function**	**Character**
Father	Leader, imposer of order, the status quo	
Mother	Nurturer, comforter, intercessor of the father	
Child	Innocent, vulnerable figure, victim, the needful one	
God	All powerful creator. The purely good one of whom all are in awe	
Devil	Destroyer. The wrench in the works of the purely good one. The despised one	

Wise Grandfather	Guru, intercessor of God, masterful transformer of Devil	
Wise Grandmother	Crone, nurturing, magic maker, balancing creation & destruction	
Trickster	Defies the status quo	
Hero	The everyday person at the highest level of virtue	
Villain	The everyday person at the lowest level of virtue	

4. Distribute the characters in the story you are writing among the generational primal archetypes using the worksheet below.

Worksheet 3: Generational Primal Archetypes for Developing Story

Story Title:		Author:
Archetype	**Metaphorical Role/ Figurative Role**	**Character**
Father	Leader, imposer of order, the status quo	
Mother	Nurturer, comforter, intercessor of the father	
Child	Innocent, vulnerable figure, victim, the needful one	
God	All powerful creator. The purely good one of whom all are in awe	
Devil	Destroyer. The wrench in the works of the purely good one. The one we all despise	
Wise Grandfather	Guru, intercessor of God, masterful transformer of Devil	
Wise Grandmother	Crone, nurturing magic maker, balancing creation & destruction	

Trickster	Defies the status quo	
Hero	The everyday person at the highest level of virtue	
Villain	The everyday person at the lowest level of virtue	

5. What elements of your story depict realistic discord within a family system?
6. Identify and analyze the negative and positive characters in your Generational Primal Archetype Worksheets above.
7. How do the characters in the Generational Primal Archetype Worksheets reflect a well-balanced tribe or pseudo-tribe? Do not confuse "balanced" with "harmonious." A balanced tribe has enough representation of archetypes to be believable regardless of how dysfunctional it is. Note that a harmonious tribe of all sister archetypes will not feel nearly as believable or satisfying as a severely dysfunctional tribe balanced with the symbols of mother, father, grandfather, etc.
    A. What other characters or elements might be conceived of to fulfill missing roles?
    B. If one character takes on more than one role, does this add to the story's vitality or confuse it?
8. How do the characters in the story you are writing reflect your own family, legends in your family, or fantasy of the ideal family?
9. How do your characters experience discord and come to terms with it through the interplay of archetypes?
    A. What is the precise mechanism?
    B. Would this be realistic in everyday life?

Chapter Two: Literary Salon

1. Check in on the developing well-being of the salon. How is the experience of the writing group impacting individuals? Is a group personality emerging?
2. Generally writing groups begin with similar age peers

mimicking siblings. If the group is mono-generational, discuss strategies to bring in multigenerational members. Seek out ways to build a group reflecting a diversity of backgrounds, age and archetypes. Overtime consider how the group is forming into a pseudo-tribe with elders, young adults and others in between.
3. Discuss what makes a tribe cohesive and healthy. What does each member consider an ideal extended family to be like? What are the similarities and differences?
4. Using the salon core study-story, have group members identify the archetypes of characters in the story.

NOTES:

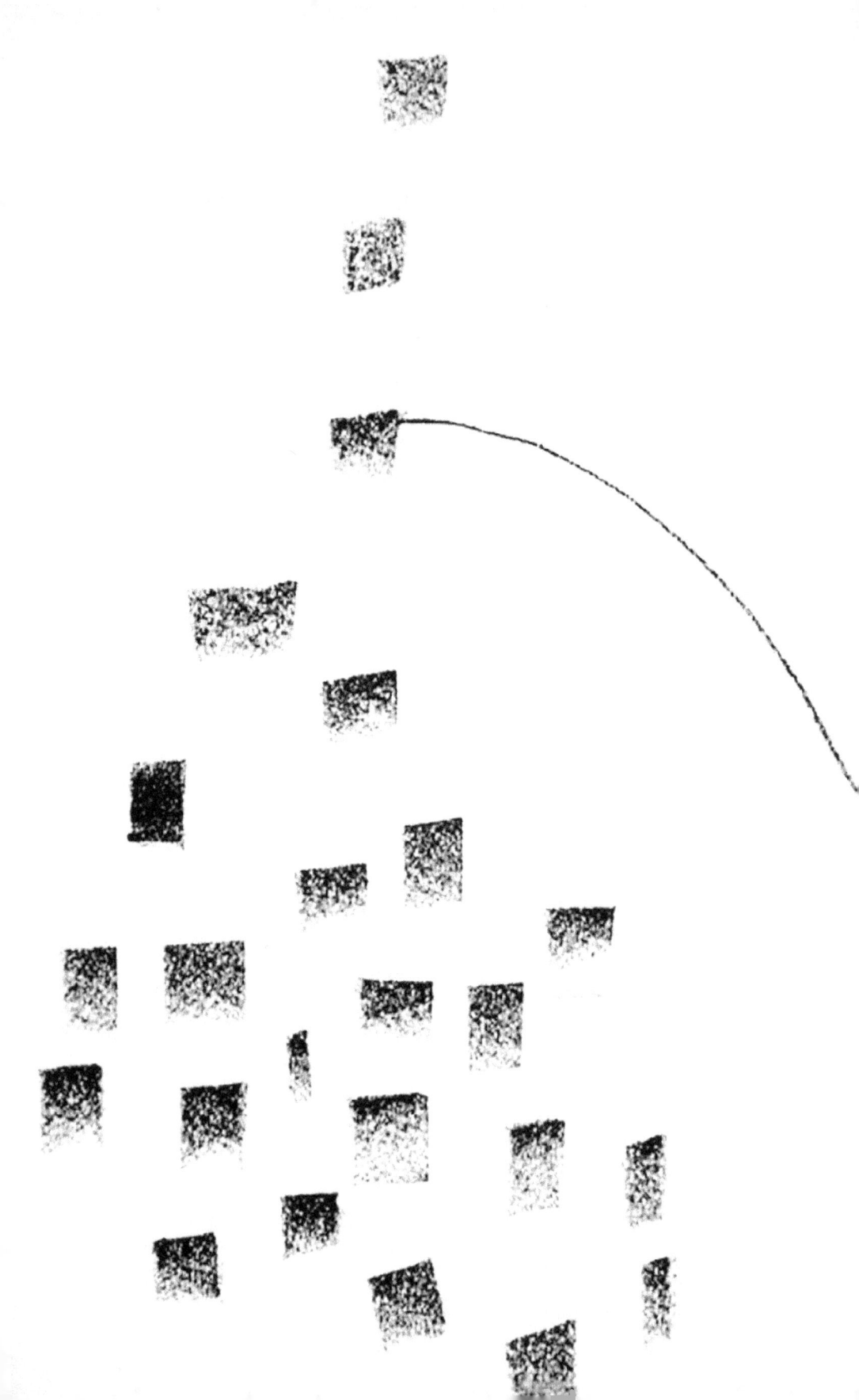

Chapter Three
The Mythological Call

The mythological call comes out of an instinctive need for us to share a moment of collective reverence with others on a deeply subconscious level. We know we are in a mystical/mythological moment when we lose ourselves in the beauty of a story, briefly lose track of time and place, and feel a sense of awe with others sharing the experience.

In such moments of collective reverence, we are in the presence of something greater than ourselves—freed from personal anguish and the stress of surviving.

The ancient Greeks thoughtfully provided for collective reverence with a sacred yearly festival of magnificent stories. While such grand pageants are important, they are not necessary for us to experience shared reverence. Even a simple story can bring it about, providing one essential element is present in the work; the hero must undergo a moment of authentic ego release through which the audience can experience a greater reality. This is often characterized as a quasi-religious experience.

From within the prison of our own egos we see only ourselves. Everything else is an interpretation of what our ego wants to see. But once the ego walls are breached and we see the reality of a greater world around us, we experience a moment of ecstasy. Unfortunately, most of us quickly fall back into the amnesia of self-centeredness thus dissolving the new vision. Then it comes again for another fleeting moment with another story granting us a peak at the ultimate reality again.

For a story to be worthy of the mythological call, writers must present the hero's momentary transcendence in a way that the audience vicariously experiences it. Stories that fail in this regard leave us disappointed and feeling exploited of time and money.

The details of character transcendence are taken up in Chapter Eight. For now, we are just touching on the general concept of it at work in the mythological call.

This ethereal idea resists easy analysis but there are a few tests we can conduct to identify where and when a story has adequately responded to the mythological call. It comes at that moment when we can no longer hold back the tear breaking away from the corner of our eyes. We feel goosebumps, lose track of time and forget we are watching a movie or reading a story. It's that point where our focus changes from wondering what happens next in the sequence of events, to wondering how the hero is going to react to these events.

The mythological call lets us re-conceptualize our real-life struggles and find new solutions via a new perspective.

Chapter Three: Individual Exercises

1. Name a few stories that have deeply touched you and identify the moments that gave you chills or brought you to tears.
2. In your study story, do you experience a moment when you turn to the person next to you to see how they are reacting?
3. Identify places in your study story where you forget you are watching/listening/reading a story and become "one" with it—where you forget yourself and your stresses?
4. How do you see the story you are writing serve the audience rather than exploit it?
5. In the story you are writing, what elements might bring about a profound emotional change in the audience's feelings about the hero?

Chapter Three: Literary Salon

1. Identify the mythological call in the group study-story.
2. Discuss to what degree the group study-story serves or exploits its audience.
3. Discuss where in the study-story the salon members largely agree that they are caught up emotionally in their reaction to the hero.
4. Is there a place in the study-story where the salon members feel collective reverence?

5. Can salon members begin to identify the possibility of collective reverence in each other's stories?
6. What kinds of life moments bring about a sense of collective reverence outside of art?
7. What kinds of discussions might engender it?

NOTES:

Chapter Four
Thinking in Balance

Of the three types of thinking that we use every day—logic, emotion, and intuition—the western world cherishes logic above all. Emotion is tolerated but denigrated whereas intuition is generally just denied. This chapter explores ways of advancing our skill with emotion and intuition.

In the west, science by means of logic is seen as the only legitimate path to discovering new knowledge and advancing human intelligence. To become smarter, we believe we must disregard intuition and suppress emotion by relegating it under logic's tight control. Yet even our most obsessive focus on logic can be easily overrun by a blast of emotion or slight pulse of intuition. When this happens, we attempt futile control of our feelings by pushing them underground where, Carl Jung tells us, they covertly and absolutely work their way back up outside of logic's radar.

The seat of our consciousness is ruled by the ego, emperor of emotion, who effortlessly manipulates logic's blind ignorance to get his way. Yet, more powerful than either logic or emotion is intuition—the mother of our intellect—shared with the physical and metaphysical world around us. Intuition works infinitely faster, more efficiently, and more powerfully than her two counterparts.

When writers bring their emotion and intuition into balance with logic, they often feel as if the writing is coming of its own accord or as if they are taking dictation from another realm. To achieve such a state, we first need to recognize how our minds function in all three modes. Only then can we consciously take steps to advance it.

Fortunately, science is not the only system of knowledge in the human world. We can also draw from other well-established traditions with rigorously developed ideas on advancing emotion and intuition. Such are the ancient spiritual traditions/systems having served their ascetics for millennia. A popular one these days is known as *mindfulness*.

Chapter Four: Individual Exercises

Exercise in Logic

In this exercise we examine how logical thought fails us when we bend it to justify poor choices. Table 1 lays out the structure of Aristotle's syllogism (see chapter nine for more details).

Table 1: Structure of the Logical Syllogism

Major Premise	A claim about a general category of something believed to be true.
Minor Premise	The specific claim drawn from the major premise narrowing the general to one specific thing.
Conclusion	The conclusion connecting the general to the specific.

We use bad logic all the time to get our way when we manipulate syllogistic reasoning. Sometimes we start with an unsound major premise, such as:

Table 2: Example of Unsound Major Premise

Major Premise (unsound)	Calories don't count on holidays.
Minor Premise	Today is a holiday.
Conclusion	Therefore, no calories count today.

Or, we might choose a minor premise that does not logically flow from the major:

Table 3: Example of Minor Premise not Following the Major

Major Premise	Butter cookies are high in calories.
Minor Premise (does not follow)	Today is a holiday.
Conclusion	Therefore, butter cookies aren't high calorie today.

Either way the logic is unsound and can lead to serious trouble.

1. Contemplate how you bend logic to legitimize a bad choice. Use the worksheet below to analyze how you justify doing something scientifically proven to be unhealthy? See Example Answers on page 103.

Worksheet 4: Syllogistic Reasoning

Major premise	
Minor Premise	
Conclusion	Therefore,

Exercises in Emotion

The first step in developing emotional skill comes with identifying and mapping how you physically react to emotional situations. For example, what happens to you physically when you stand up in front of a crowd to give a speech? Even the most logically written speech can quickly become a sheer emotional experience in such a situation.

2. The outer body experiences. Rate how the surface/skin of your body reacts to an emotional situation.

Worksheet 5: Outer Body Experiences

	Low	High
Perspiration	1-------------------------------	10
Twitching	1-------------------------------	10
Flushing	1-------------------------------	10
Blotching	1-------------------------------	10
Describe reactions with your skin:		

3. The inner body experiences. Rate how your inner body reacts to the emotional situations.

Worksheet 6: Inner Body Experiences

	Low	High
Trembling hands/arms	1	10
Trembling jaw	1	10
Trembling knees/legs	1	10
Trembling shoulders	1	10
Nausea	1	10
Chest breathing	1	10

Describe your inner body reaction:

4. Face facts. How does your face, tongue, and throat react?

Worksheet 7: Face Facts

	Low	High
Voice raises	1	10
Speaking too fast	1	10
Breathy voice	1	10
Tongue clumsy/heavy	1	10
Teeth clench/jaw tight	1	10

Describe the changes in your throat/jaw/and face (these affect your voice and sound production:

5. Core Reactions. How does your central nervous system and cognitive processing react?

Worksheet 8: Core Reactions

	Low	**High**
Heart rate increases	1	10
Memory blanks out	1	10
Feeling dissociative	1	10
Color and sound changes	1	10
Difficulty keeping focused	1	10
Heightened sense of awareness	1	10
Feeling "jumpy"	1	10

Describe some feelings associated with your central nervous system and cognitive processing functions.

6. Emotional Reactions. How do your emotions affect how you feel about yourself?

Worksheet 9: Emotional Reactions

	Low	**High**
Feeling inadequate	1	10
Fear of being boring	1	10
Fear of looking dumb	1	10
Fear of showing fear	1	10
Depressed at self	1	10
Angry at self	1	10
Happy at self	1	10

Describe your emotional reactions:

Exercises in Intuition

These final exercises address intuition or what we call "sudden insight." This is the mode of thinking that brings solutions to complex problems all at once. It functions infinitely faster than understanding through our senses or use of language. While we cannot "will" this type of thought into being, we can still create favorable situations for it to arise.

Rollo May suggests that intuitive thinking comes at an "in between point" between work and rest. It's that moment when we are getting on the bus that we suddenly know how to write the term paper. Or we might be just stepping out on the jogging trail when a breakthrough comes. For many, it often comes first thing in the morning, in the transition between sleeping and waking.

7. Keep a journal of your experience of sudden insight guided by the following questions:
    A. Where were you when it happened?
    B. What time of day was it?
    C. What were you doing just before the idea came?
    D. How long did it take for the idea to completely unfold in your mind?
    E. Write out the complete idea.
    F. Compare how long it took to grasp the idea in your mind as it arrived, to how long it took to translate it in the logical realm of language.
8. Become more aware of your periods of transition between work and rest or play. Do you notice ideas coming more easily in such transitions? If so, contemplate the way you think in these transitions compared to the way you think in just work or just rest.

Chapter Four: Literary Salon

1. How have members experienced having sudden realization? What types of ideas or solutions to complex problems have arrived?
2. Discuss moments of transition between work and rest. Have salon members experienced sudden insight during these moments?

3. Discuss a well-known person or people who demonstrate the qualities of "golden era" thinking. While no great golden eras can be identified presently, some communities do have cultural moments when there seems to be a balance of the three modes of thought. Perhaps the salon is one such group. What groups or communities can salon members identify that have moments of "Golden Era Thinking"?
4. Discuss what would signal the beginning of a new golden age for an entire society.

NOTES:

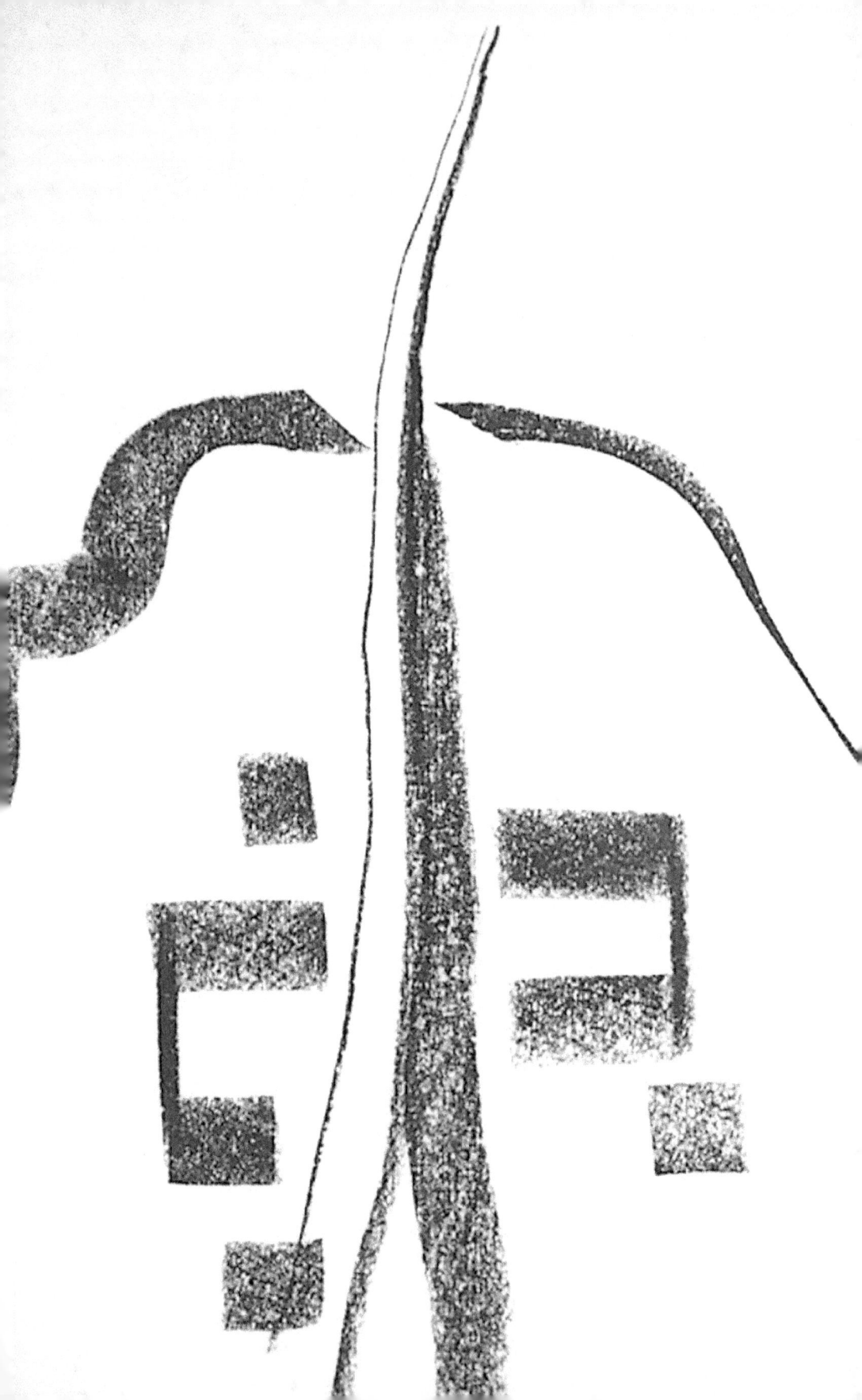

Chapter Five
Awakening to Language

Chapter Five explores the distinction between written and spoken English and how moving between the two can easily trigger writer's block.

Back in the solid days of modernity, a few forms of standard spoken English were selected, taught, and carefully regulated. Oxford English became the canon for Great Britain while Midwestern English rose to the standard for the United States. The hundreds of other "non-standard" varieties were tolerated but consigned to inferior status, with their speakers marked as belonging to a subclass of "proper" culture. The further you were on the periphery from the standard, the lower your social station was perceived to be.

However, no tolerance for variation was allowed when it came to written English. There existed one and only one standard per country which was rigidly kept in place by the English teacher's merciless red pen. Then came postmodernity when rules gave way to an explosion of chaos that became the Internet. Speakers using those hundreds of varieties of English began texting away using print to convey their native spoken form. Teachers are still trying diligently, but futilely, to preserve a very different language than the one we speak. Written English differs from the spoken in diction, syntax, lexicon, and grammatical rules. Trying to switch between any two different languages can easily trigger false starts, hesitations, and lots of, "uhm."

A first step in avoiding writer's block is simply to recognize that you are shifting into another language. It's difficult enough just taking an idea from the realm of pure intuition and translating it into language at all; but when we must further translate it into a language that we never speak and only use when writing, the task of composing becomes even harder. And with the massive shift to using spoken language in printed form online, standard written English is becoming ever more foreign.

But it doesn't work the other way around. We cannot get away with speaking in the written form. An easy place to spot this is in a public speaking class where inevitably a student trying to take a shortcut will attempt to use a term paper written for another class as the text for a speech. Within a few seconds the shaking student standing at the podium realizes that everyone knows that the paper being read was drafted in written language, and a failing grade is about to follow.

The increasing use of printed spoken language in place of standard written causes writers to lose fluency in the written form and naturally triggers a widening epidemic of writers' block.

However, once you recognize written English as a separate language and engage it as such, you can *mindfully* switch between languages—which often breaks the block. When we don't realize a transition is happening, we can end up lingering in the transitory space between the two lexical worlds, making it hard to land solidly enough in either one to compose a story. When this happens, we tend to think that the problem is with our creativity rather than the very real possibility that it might just be a failed neurological connection in the language area of our brains.

But it's not just structure that gets lost between the written and spoken forms of English. There is also a dynamic difference in the sound of the two. As we become more monotone in using only one form of the language, the melody of our writing also flattens.

Chapter Five Individual Exercises

These exercises are best done in the order they are given.
1. Pick a passage from a finely crafted piece of literature and translate it into spoken English. Audio record yourself reading both and compare the two for differences in word choice and grammatical structure.
2. Repeat #1 with one of your own written works.
3. Obtain a recording of *Beowulf* in Old English. Select a three-minute segment to capture. Do the same for a story by Chaucer and another from Shakespeare and put the three into a single file, chronologically.
4. Listen to the full nine minutes as the language moves from old English to Middle English to Shakespeare. Move beyond

the limitation of sound by observing the patterns of the sine waves of these recordings. (Audacity is a free, open source program for this: www.audacityteam.org).
5. Add to this file one to two minutes of three or four other similar modern languages such as Friesian, Scots or Irish Gaelic, or Swedish. Passively listen to all of them in one session as you focus on feeling the rhythm and melody of the sound. Notice the patterns of the sine waves with these languages as well.
6. Choose a paragraph from a classic 19th century novel written in English and copy the paragraph by hand using pen and paper. Translate the paragraph by hand into your everyday variety of spoken English (your home variety is preferred to standard English).
7. Repeat the exercise #6 using a 18th century novel.
8. Repeat the exercise #6 using a 17th century novel.
9. Briefly discuss some of the similarities and differences in the written form of these three eras.
10. Did you notice a change in your printed everyday spoken language as you moved between the three translations? Does your home language seem a little different between these forms?
11. Discuss the difficulty or ease you experienced in making your translations. Was it hard to change from written to spoken? Was the effort to translate equal or was one era more difficult than another?
12. Audio record a few paragraphs of your own writing. Listen to it and reflect on what it feels like to hear your own work in your own voice in standard written English. What do you like and not like about it?

Advanced Work

13. Create an audio file with five minutes each of the following (in the order they are given):
    A. Anglo-Saxon English (i.e. Beowulf)
    B. Middle English (i.e. Chaucer)
    C. Elizabethan English (i.e. Langland or Shakespeare)

D. Modern Irish Gaelic
   E. Modern Scots Gaelic
   F. Frisian
   G. Dutch
   H. Afrikaans
   I. Swedish
   J. Hebridean Scott's English
14. Passively listen to the audio recordings as you would background music, while you perform a physical task such as going for a walk or tidying the house.
15. Note your impressions of the sound of the languages. What did the sounds remind you of? What thoughts did they bring to mind? Describe a brief image that crossed your mind as you were listening.

Chapter Five Literary Salon

1. Discuss group members' experience in switching from spoken to written English. Are there common struggles?
2. Discuss the impact of social media on writing and on the written language.
3. If the salon is intergenerational, discuss changes in the language that older members have experienced in their lifetimes.
4. Have the group choose one piece of fine literature and each member translate the same brief passage into spoken English. How do the passages differ? No two are likely to be alike, even if everyone speaks the same home language.
5. Identify varieties of English that some group members cannot understand and discuss the experience of exploring/encountering them.
6. As a game, help each other translate one paragraph of each writer's work into old English, Middle English, or Shakespearean English.

NOTES:

Chapter Six
Delilah's Scissors

Contemporary storytelling in the western world is slipping further into a latent dependency on filler words and profanity as ever more writers avoid the hard work of skillfully expressing emotion. Profanity, clichés, and other filler language has a place but its sloppy use weakens our writing. The aim of this chapter is to help writers recognize, understand, and advance their emotional intelligence through the practice of language.

Shakespeare wrote with such precision that he conveyed a characters' emotions through dialogue alone, without stage directions telling actors how to deliver the line (i.e. "sadly" or "angrily"). He reserved stage directions for entries, exits, or significant actions such as Hamlet running his sword through the bed curtain and killing Polonius. Few living writers in the west today have such ability to convey emotion. The scientific stranglehold of modernity, which saw emotion as a threat from our ancient animal nature, swiftly stunted the potential of our emotional intelligence. An obsession with logic forbade us to openly experience emotions deeply, celebrate their beauty, shape them, or consciously advance skill with them. We remain largely ignorant of our emotions, often smash blindly into them, and are left writhing in the torment of their fallout.

In our era, the focus on emotion is one of *control* and *suppression* rather than skillful advancement. We've become afraid of ourselves and cower in meaningless filler words that sound tough, brave, or scary but convey only weakness to those who know what is really happening. Be it profanity or cliché, filler words smother our genius and deny literary magic.

The first step to empowering our writing is to take back command of our language with the hard work of recognizing exactly what we are feeling and why. It begins with looking at what happens to our feelings when we send them into language.

Chapter Six Individual Exercises

1. Pick a few minutes in your study story with particularly heavy use of profanity, cliché, gesture, or filler words. Translate the emotion behind it. What exactly does a given word or gesture convey?
2. Revise the passage with more precise language (or action). What is the effect?
3. Audio record yourself in a casual conversation with someone, especially someone with whom you feel most linguistically lazy.
    A. Transcribe verbatim about five minutes of the conversation.
    B. Analyze your use of filler words and profanity. What are you really trying to say? What is the exact feeling behind the lazy words?
4. Begin keeping a record of the curse word, gestures, or the substitutes for them that you regularly use.
    A. Make a table with four columns.
       - In the first column note the word or gesture.
       - In the second column, define what it means to you.
       - In the third column, note what triggers it.
       - In the last column, identify the emotion behind it.
    B. Analyze the feelings behind a given word or gesture. Were you able to identify them all? What difficulties did you face with this exercise?
5. Return to the audio recording you made of yourself reading your own work aloud from Chapter Five.
    A. Make a new recording of the passage but this time let each vowel and consonant have its full measure. Think of the sound of your words as if they were notes of music that if weakly struck would ruin the song. *Feel* the words. Give each of them, *even the blandest of them*, power—as if they were the most sacred or worst profane. The point is to use the sound of the language to convey the deeper feeling.
    B. Listen to the recording and reflect on it.
    C. Rewrite it as you are so moved.

D. Note what has changed in the revision.
   E. Re-record the revision, listen to it, and reflect on the changes.
      - How did they make you feel?
      - How did it alter your thinking about the piece?
      - Did the revision make a difference in the beauty of the language?
   F. Listen and re-record again as you like until you are satisfied with it.
   G. Once the polished piece is done return to the original recording and compare the two. Do you hear a difference in the timber and resonance of your voice? In the power of your language? Seek that level in your daily speech.
6. Another way to explore the dynamics of your language is to convert the spoken passage to sine waves and experiment with making the waves higher, wider, or smoother in search of more rhythmic movement.

Advanced work

7. Abstain from profanity and filler words for six months while keeping a journal of your experience. In the journal make note of:
   A. How you use non-verbal communication.
      - Do you use more silence now?
      - Has your use of eye contact changed?
      - Has your use of space changed to reflect your state of mind?
   B. What the loss of this language forces you to do. How do you compensate?
   C. The changes in your use of language.
   D. How your understanding of your emotions is changing.
   E. Changes in your enunciation to convey what profanity had done before.

Chapter Six Literary Salon

1. Share a scene from a popular or award-winning film with little or no profanity.
2. Discuss the effect of the story without profanity. How does the writer convey powerful emotion?
3. Share a scene from a popular or award-winning film with abundant profanity. Compare the two films in discussion.
4. As a group, revise a short scene from the profanity laden film to use more meaningful language.
   A. Does doing so diminish the work? If so how?
   B. If it enhances the work, how?
5. Listen to several minutes of *Beowulf* together.
   A. Comment on the sound and feeling of the language.
   B. What seems familiar with the language of the modern day?
   C. What words feel like profanity?
   D. Which ones feel like filler words?
6. Translate a few of the words that stand out as powerful by using an online translator such as:
   https://lingojam.com/OldEnglishTranslator
   http://www.majstro.com/dictionaries/English-Old%20English
   https://www.oldenglishtranslator.co.uk/
   https://www.freelang.net/online/old_english.php?lg=gb
7. Discuss some changes in the social acceptance of words that have happened in your lifetimes.

NOTES:

Chapter Seven
The Plot Situation

Chapter Seven takes us into the world of story plots through the lens of the French writer Georges Polti and his legendary book *The Thirty-Six Dramatic Situations*. Polti tells us these basic plots of human life were drawn from a manuscript originating centuries before and passed down through the hands of writing masters. The work was translated from French into an archaic form of English (it was likely in Italian first then possibly German before the French). It has been simplified and modernized in *The Universal Grammar of Story*™.

Chapter Seven Individual Exercises

1. On the worksheet below:
   A. Choose the plot situation that best fits your study story.
   B. Contemplate three or four other plot situations and consider how each would change the story.
   C. Associate as many of the remaining plot situations as possible to:
      - Other stories you have seen or read,
      - Stories from contemporary events,
      - Stories from history,
      - Stories from your real-life experiences, or
      - Stories from the experiences of others.

Worksheet 10: The 36 Dramatic Situations for Study Story and Others

Plot Situation	Story Title
1. Abduction	
2. Adultery	
3. All Ruined for Passion	

4. Ambition	
5. An Enemy Loved	
6. Bold Adventure/Enterprise	
7. Conflict with God	
8. Crime of Love	
9. Crime of Vengeance	
10. Deliverance	
11. Disaster	
12. Discovering Dishonor of a Loved One	
13. Fatal Misjudgment	
14. Hatred of a Relative	
15. Humble Appeal for Aid	
16. Killing of Unrecognized Relative	
17. Loss of Loved Ones	
18. Madness	
19. Mistaken Jealousy	
20. Mistaken Judgment	
21. Murderous Adultery	
22. Needful Sacrifice of a Loved One	
23. Object to be Gained	
24. Obstacles to Love	
25. Pursuit	
26. Recovery of a Lost One	
27. Remorse	
28. Revolt	
29. Rivalry between Superior and Inferior	
30. Rivalry of a Relative	
31. Self-sacrifice for a Relative	
32. Self-sacrifice for an Ideal	
33. Solve the Riddle	
34. Unintended Crimes of Love	
35. Vengeance for Family	
36. Victim of Misfortune	

2. Using the worksheet below for your emerging story:
   A. Choose the dramatic situation that best fits.
   B. Consider another three or four situations and contemplate how each would change the story.
   C. Find one or two other situations that would work as subplots between the main characters and minor ones, or among minor characters.

Worksheet 11: The 36 Dramatic Situations for Emerging Story

Plot Situation	Story Title
1. Abduction	
2. Adultery	
3. All Ruined for Passion	
4. Ambition	
5. An Enemy Loved	
6. Bold Adventure/Enterprise	
7. Conflict with God	
8. Crime of Love	
9. Crime of Vengeance	
10. Deliverance	
11. Disaster	
12. Discovering Dishonor of a Loved One	
13. Fatal Misjudgment	
14. Hatred of a Relative	
15. Humble Appeal for Aid	
16. Killing of Unrecognized Relative	
17. Loss of Loved Ones	
18. Madness	
19. Mistaken Jealousy	
20. Mistaken Judgment	
21. Murderous Adultery	
22. Needful Sacrifice of a Loved One	
23. Object to be Gained	

24. Obstacles to Love	
25. Pursuit	
26. Recovery of a Lost One	
27. Remorse	
28. Revolt	
29. Rivalry between Superior and Inferior	
30. Rivalry of a Relative	
31. Self-sacrifice for a Relative	
32. Self-sacrifice for an Ideal	
33. Solve the Riddle	
34. Unintended Crimes of Love	
35. Vengeance for Family	
36. Victim of Misfortune	

3. Do you think that some of the plot situations are outdated and no longer useful? If so, explain why.

Advanced Work

4. Consider how each of all 36 situations would change your story. Some will likely be so ridiculous that a drama or horror story would flip into a buffoonish satire or slapstick comedy. Contemplate the ridiculous and do not limit your efforts to plots that make sense. This is a brainstorming exercise meant to open your mind to as many twists as possible for your characters. You may well find subplots emerging here, so contemplate all 36 with diligence. Try to keep this exercise easy and playful even as it is demanding.
5. For plots that do not fit the main story in any way, briefly explain why.
6. Contemplate any new discoveries you have made as the story traveled through each situation.
7. Using the worksheet below, find potential subplots for your story. One way to do this is by assigning all the characters to a plot situation of their own. This becomes their "theme"

or "mantra," granting them purpose beyond a robotic or meaningless function for the "real" characters. All characters need to be real and finding each one's dramatic situation is what makes them so.

Worksheet 12: The 36 Dramatic Situations for Subplots and Minor Characters

Plot Situation	Story Title
1. Abduction	
2. Adultery	
3. All Ruined for Passion	
4. Ambition	
5. An Enemy Loved	
6. Bold Adventure/Enterprise	
7. Conflict with God	
8. Crime of Love	
9. Crime of Vengeance	
10. Deliverance	
11. Disaster	
12. Discovering Dishonor of a Loved One	
13. Fatal Misjudgment	
14. Hatred of a Relative	
15. Humble Appeal for Aid	
16. Killing of Unrecognized Relative	
17. Loss of Loved Ones	
18. Madness	
19. Mistaken Jealousy	
20. Mistaken Judgment	
21. Murderous Adultery	
22. Needful Sacrifice of a Loved One	
23. Object to be Gained	
24. Obstacles to Love	

25. Pursuit	
26. Recovery of a Lost One	
27. Remorse	
28. Revolt	
29. Rivalry between Superior and Inferior	
30. Rivalry of a Relative	
31. Self-sacrifice for a Relative	
32. Self-sacrifice for an Ideal	
33. Solve the Riddle	
34. Unintended Crimes of Love	
35. Vengeance for Family	
36. Victim of Misfortune	

Chapter Seven Literary Salon

1. Discuss the relevance of the 36 plot situations for contemporary stories. Should they be altered? How so?
2. Contemplate the role of the seven deadly sins of the western world as they might fit into Polti's 36 Situations. What is the role of morality here?
3. Which plot situation best fits the group study story?
4. Which might fit the subplots?
5. What would be the most ridiculous situation for the study story? Enjoy a good laugh at turning the story into a satire (or new satire) by forcing it into an outrageously different plot situation.

NOTES:

Chapter Eight
Opposition and Conflict

Chapter Eight examines the fundamental role of the hero as one undergoing transformation on behalf of the greater society. Such transformation can only happen through opposition and conflict.

Heroes exist as role models of humility—the sole path for social and spiritual evolution. The other characters in the story exist to facilitate the hero's transformation. Of these, none is more central than the villain/antihero. Until the arrival of the villain, the hero lives in a self-imposed prison built of an increasingly intolerable status quo erected and held in place by the hero's ego. The villain comes to set the hero free by crashing into the status quo.

Creating heroes and villains worthy of strong social role models begins with the simple selection of opposing adjectives to describe them.

Heroes and villains begin their stories as opposing points on a shared continuum. The further they are from one another on that continuum at the outset, the stronger the story becomes. Little by little over the course of the story they move from one pole to the other. For one brief magical moment they meet in the middle, existing on the same point before passing each other to complete the journey to the opposite side.

Chapter Eight: Individual Exercises

For your study story:
1. Identify the hero and explain how you know this is the true hero.
2. What is the hero's defining adjective? (See Unity of Opposite Pairs, Table 16, page 104.
3. Briefly describe your experience in choosing the hero's adjective. Did you struggle with it?
4. Repeat #1-3 for the antihero.

5. Discuss how the antonym of the hero describes the antihero or vice versa.
6. How do the defining adjectives of the hero and antihero form a strong unity of opposites? (See Table 16 on page 104 for a guiding list).
7. What conflict inevitably arises from these opposites?
8. What characteristics do the hero and antihero share?

For the story you are writing:
9. Repeat exercises #1-8 for your story.
10. Using the worksheet below, identify the points of polarity and commonality between the hero and antihero. See Example Answer, Table 17, page 106.

Worksheet 13: Hero-Villain Polarity

Hero --- Antihero

Defining Adjective **Defining Adjective**

Characteristic Traits of the Hero: _____

Characteristic Traits of the antihero: _____

Characteristics they have in common: _____

Adjective of common trait between the two: _____

Mark the point where the adjective of commonality falls on the continuum of polarity. Does it fall balanced in the center? Or is it more toward the side of one character or the other?

Adjective of Commonality
Hero --- Antihero

Hero's Adjective   **Common Adjective**   **Antihero's Adjective**

11. Did working through the polarity of hero and antihero cause you to rethink who might be the authentic hero or antihero in your story?
12. Egri guides us in the incremental movement characters take psychologically as they move from one state of being to its opposite. Use the worksheet below to contemplate the incremental steps your hero must take to move from one pole of the unity of opposites to the other. See Example Answer, Table 18, page 107.

Worksheet 14: Incremental Polar Movement

From:	To:
1	
2	
3	
4	
5	
6	
7	
8	
9	
10	
11	
12	
13	
14	

Advanced Work

13. Change does not commence without a trigger. What external events in your story might help trigger the change? Refine the steps you created above and use the worksheet below to contemplate the sequence of events preceding or coinciding with the change.

Worksheet 15: Events Triggering Polar Movement

From: To:	Events that could trigger the shift
1	
2	
3	
4	
5	
6	
7	
8	
9	
10	
11	
12	
13	
14	

14. Now it's time to weave the supporting characters into the triggering events. Return to your worksheet of supporting characters from Chapter One, indicating their positive/negative relationship to the hero. Use this to complete the worksheet below to contemplate how each might nudge the hero toward change. The nudge may be very slight but when all the characters do so, the cumulative effect is profound. This exercise also helps evolve the supporting characters.

Worksheet 16: Collective Forces Triggering Hero's Transformation

How do the supporting characters nudge the hero toward transcendence?		
Character Name and Role	How they nudge	Event triggering a nudge

15. In a single sentence, explain how the conflict drives the hero's transformation.
16. Looking at your own life, how might villains have pushed you toward transformation? What unity of opposites might have played out?
17. In what way is the story you are writing free from stereotyping constraint?
    A. What elements of the story might allow it to transcend time, race, and culture?
    B. What is the core, the universal story, that will allow it to become meaningful into alien cultures and the distant future?

Chapter Eight: Literary Salon

1. Discuss the unity of opposites for the salon study film.
   A. How the hero and antihero move toward each other.
   B. How the unity of opposites gives rise to the conflict.
2. Can the group identify a moment in the salon study story when the hero shifts from trying to achieve the goal at the story's beginning to something greater?
3. What is the metaphor of transcendence in the salon study story?
4. Consider how real-life figures have moved or appear to be moving toward their opposite in time.
5. Discuss the existing or potential unity of opposites in the stories being written by salon members.
6. How does the unity of opposites in the stories of the salon members point the hero toward humility?

Chapter Nine
Story Chemistry

Story chemistry within the Universal Grammar of Story builds on the logic of Aristotle as adapted by Edward Price and Bernard Grebanier. The chemistry is composed of explosive elements in the relationship between hero and antihero, which when combined, leads to a logical, inevitable, and believable outcome.

The chemical elements of characters are composed of their strengths and vulnerabilities, as well as the stakes hanging in the tension between them.

Chapter Nine: Individual Exercises

1. Use your study story to complete the worksheet below for the five elements of the hero's proposition. See Example Answers, Table 19, page 108.

Worksheet 17: The Five Elements for Study Story

The Five Elements of the Hero's Proposition	
Title:	Author:
A. Hero's Inner Conflict	An inner weakness (or vulnerability) in tension with an opposing need which causes the hero constant trouble in life
B. Unity of Opposites	A single adjective describing the hero, and its antonym for the antihero

C.	Destabilizing Situation	A deteriorating situation triggering a psychological journey forcing the hero to confront and overcome the inner weakness
D.	The Stakes	The risk of losing something of life and death importance to the hero
E.	Potential Resolution to the Conflict	An idea appearing in the introduction to the story that hints at a way to solve the dilemma

2. Use Worksheet 18 below to analyze the five elements of the hero's proposition for the story <u>you are writing.</u>

Worksheet 18: Five Elements of the Hero's Proposition for Your Story

The Five Elements of the Hero's Proposition	
Title:	
A. Hero's Inner Conflict	
B. Unity of Opposites	
C. Destabilizing Situation	
D. The Stakes	
E. Potential Resolution to the Conflict	

3. Explain how the antihero blocks the hero's strength, and threatens the hero's vulnerability, in both your study story and the one you are writing. See Example Answer on page 108.
4. With the answers to the above questions, formulate a State of Affairs for your study story. See Example Answers, Table 20, page 109.

Worksheet 19: *State of Affairs for Study Story*

Title:		Author:	
_____, a _____ who is _____,			
Hero	Unity of Opposites		Inner Conflict/vulnerability
facing _____			
the Stakes	learns/discovers/finds		Destabilizing Context
Antihero	Unity of Opposites for Antihero		Potential Resolution

5. Formulate a State of Affairs for the story you are writing.

Worksheet 20: *State of Affairs for Developing Story*

Story Title:			
_____, a _____ who is _____,			
Hero	Unity of Opposites		Inner Conflict/vulnerability
facing _____			
the Stakes	learns/discovers/finds		Destabilizing Context
Antihero	Unity of Opposites for Antihero		Potential Resolution

Answer questions 4-14 for your study story, then repeat them for the story you are writing:

6. What happens at The Challenge?
7. Describe what makes The Challenge startling in its exceptionality, unexpectedness, and daring.
8. How is The Challenge an act of free will of the hero?
9. How is The Challenge a momentary lapse with permanent consequences?
10. How is The Challenge an act of vulnerability to the hero's ego?
11. How is The Challenge irreversible?

12. How does The Challenge reflect the tension between the hero's strength and vulnerability?
13. What is the Dramatic Question sparked by The Challenge?
14. Who is the third character?
15. For your Study Story, formulate a full Proposition using the worksheet below. For detailed examples, see Chapter 9 of the core book *The Universal Grammar of Story: An Author's Guide to Writing for the Soul of the World*.

Worksheet 21: Full Proposition with prompts for Study Story

State of Affairs	(Copy from worksheet above)
The Challenge	_____(Hero)_____(takes an action) to/with_____(secondary character).
The Dramatic Question	Will_____ (hero) overcome_____ (vulnerability) and_____with _____(antihero)? *change in relationship*
The Climax	_____(hero)_____(an action) with/to_____(third character).

16. For the story you are writing, build a full Proposition using the worksheet below.

Worksheet 22: State of Affairs for Developing Story

State of Affairs	(Copy from worksheet above)
The Challenge	_____(Hero)_____(takes an action) to/with_____(secondary character).

The Dramatic Question	Will_____ (hero) overcome _____ (vulnerability) and_____ with_____ (antihero)? change in relationship
The Climax	_____(hero)_____(an action) with/to_____(third character).

Advanced Work

17. Build a Proposition for the antihero of the story you are writing.

Worksheet 23: State of Affairs for the Antihero of Developing Story

Proposition for _____ for _____	
Antihero Title	
State of Affairs	
The Challenge	
The Dramatic Question	
The Climax	

If you have difficulty writing the fully manifested Proposition in a linear sequence (as most people do), then approach it by working backwards beginning with the dramatic question.

Chapter Nine Literary Salon

1. As a group, identify the five elements of the story proposition for the salon study story.
2. Create the Proposition.
3. Identify The Challenge.
4. Who does the group see as the third character?
5. What triggers the climax?
6. Using an ongoing story in the news, create a completed proposition for the main person involved and forecast how the story might resolve itself in the future based on that proposition.

NOTES:

Chapter Ten
The Structure of Timing

Chapter Ten takes up the sequence of events and exact proportions of timing giving stories their rhythm.

The milestones of timing provide a map and a timetable for the story's unfolding. Very few people are aware of the role of timing but nearly everyone feels it go awry when the milestones are missed or poorly placed.

The exercises below will result in a five-page treatment for your story.

Chapter Ten Individual Exercises

1. Identify the milestones of timing for your study story using the worksheet below. See Example Answers, Table 21, page 110.

Worksheet 24: Timing Milestones for Study Story

Timing Milestone	Expected % of story	Actual % of story	Description
The Introductory Event	1-10		
Introduction of the Hero	1-3		
Introduction of the Antihero	1-5		

Completion of Introduction of Supporting Characters	12-20		
Introduction of the Stakes	5-15		
The Point of No Return/The Challenge	20		
The Doldrums (either a moment of genius or the beginning of the story's collapse).	33		
Midpoint Reversal of Fortunes	50		
All Hope Is Lost	66		
The Climax	66-67		
The Miracle	66-67		
Resolution	68-end		

2. Use the worksheet below to draft a rough concept of timing milestones for the story you are writing.

Worksheet 25: Concept of Emerging Story Timing

Timing Milestone	Expected % of story	Description
The Introductory Event	1-10	
Introduction of the Hero	1-3	
Introduction of the Antihero	1-5	
Completion of Introduction of Supporting Characters	12-20	
Introduction of the Stakes	5-15	
The Point of No Return/The Challenge	20	

The Doldrums (a moment of genius or the beginning of the story's collapse).	33	
Midpoint Reversal of Fortunes	50	
All Hope Is Lost	66	
The Climax	66-67	
The Miracle	66-67	
Resolution	68- end	

3. Briefly describe your experience developing the timing sheet. Did it generate new ideas for your story?
4. Draft a page of narrative summarizing the introduction to your story. Include the following elements which must unfold in the first ten percent of the story proper:

A. Introduce the destabilizing event launching the story and foreshadowing the central crisis to come.
B. Introduce the hero in perfect depiction of the defining adjective. Show the hero reacting to the event by intensely avoiding or denying the inner vulnerability.
C. Introduce the antihero through the destabilizing event. Establish the unity of opposites by showing how the antihero is a threat to the hero's vulnerability.
D. Introduce the remaining characters by showing how their lives suffer because of the vulnerability of the hero.
5. Draft a second page of narrative that completes the introduction. Include the remaining elements for the second ten percent of the story:
A. The stakes for the hero.
B. The stakes for the antihero.
C. The stakes for the community.
D. Any additional threats or risks.
E. Bring closure to the introduction with any other symbols or props that will become crucial to the story.
6. Draft a third page of narrative describing:
A. The Challenge and how the characters react to it.
B. The disorienting world the hero is thrown into after The Challenge as things go awry and forward moving attempts dead end or backfire.
C. The story will naturally begin to reach a lull at the Doldrums, near the thirty-three percent mark, which is precisely where you must launch your genius with your best lines. Contemplate a poetic moment foreshadowing the point of All Hope is Lost to come. Things must either get better for the hero or worse. If they stagnate, the story will collapse.
D. Describe the midpoint reversal. How does it impact the dream the hero was pursuing at The Challenge? The reversal moves in the opposite direction of what happened at the thirty-three percent mark.
E. From the midpoint reversal to the sixty-six percent mark, show the dream slowly but continuously collapsing.

7. Write a fourth page of narrative contemplating All Hope is Lost. Describe:
   A. The arrival of All Hope is Lost and the collapse of the dream the hero held at The Challenge.
   B. The powerful moment when the hero experiences genuine humility by surrendering the ego's desire.
   C. The climax, and how the third character acts as witness to the transformation of the hero.
   D. The miracle the hero is given for ego release.
8. Write a fifth page of narrative contemplating how the story will resolve with the major characters coming together and to validate the hero's transformation.

Chapter Ten: Literary Salon

1. Reflect on moments that might constitute a Point of No Return for the journey of a generation.
2. What questions did such a change generate?
3. Have the salon work together to mark the timing of the salon study story.
4. Choose a real-life event from the past and discuss whether the experience of the central figure in that event fit or did not fit into the timing of the Universal Grammar of Story.
5. Choose a real-life event that is now beginning to unfold. Using the timing of the Universal Grammar of Story, what predictions can the group make as to what might happen for the central figure of the event?

NOTES:

Chapter Eleven
Joseph Campbell's Hero's Journey

Chapter Eleven shakes off our hard-won grasp of the logical core narrative theories with a sharp turn into the ethereal world of mythology. Here, writers must surrender logical control to the will of intuition. Mythological elements come of their own accord and effortlessly resist the writer's best predetermined calculations for the hero's journey. All we can do is sit back and recognize where the mythology has decided to start.

The timing of the hero's journey does not follow the same fixed proportions as does the core narrative theory (chapter ten). The beginning of the mythology and the placement of its milestones differs from story to story. Sometimes they match up with the core timing and sometimes not. There is, however, one consistently shared common point: The Belly of the Whale in the hero's journey falls at the same point as All Hope is Lost in the core theory of timing. But the beginning of the hero's inner journey might start anywhere up to that point—perhaps on the first page or not until just before the two-thirds mark of the story near All Hope is Lost.

Chapter Eleven Individual Exercises

Answer the following questions for your study story, then repeat them for the story you are writing.
1. How is the everyday world portrayed?
2. What is the misery the people experience that requires a hero to come?
3. How is the call to adventure portrayed?
4. How is the call rejected?
5. What form does supernatural aid take?
6. How is the threshold crossed into the unknown zone?
7. What suffering does the hero go through in the Belly of the Whale?
8. What is symbolized in the "elixir of the gods" that the hero

brings back in your study story?
9. How does the outer physical journey compare to the inner psychological one for the hero?
10. Using worksheet 26, analyze the hero's journey for your study story. Remember, the hero's journey is ultimately a psychological one, freeing the hero from the tyranny of the unrestrained ego. So, while the study story might depict an outer journey of intense adventure into deep space, it is the inner journey that we examine through mythology. This journey is triggered by the antihero.

Worksheet 26: Hero's Journey for Study Story

	Campbell's Hero's Journey		Action by Hero	Effect on Hero's Ego
Departure	Ordinary World			
	Call to Adventure			
	Refusal of the Call			
	Crossing the Threshold			
	Supernatural Aid			
	Belly of the Whale—the death of the ego			
Initiation	Road of Trials—making certain the ego is dead			
	Meeting with the Godhead	1. Sacred Marriage to the Goddess, or		
		2. Atonement with the Father, or		
		3. Apotheosis		
	The Ultimate Boon—the Elixir of Life Received			
Return	Return to the Ordinary World with the Elixir			
	Master of Two Worlds—Heaven and Earth			

11. Use worksheet 27 to repeat #10 for the story you are writing.

Worksheet 27: Hero's Journey for Emerging Story

	Campbell's Hero's Journey		Action by Hero	Effect on Hero's Ego
Departure	Ordinary World			
Departure	Call to Adventure			
Departure	Refusal of the Call			
Departure	Crossing the Threshold			
Departure	Supernatural Aid			
Initiation	Belly of the Whale—the death of the ego			
Initiation	Road of Trials—making certain the ego is dead			
Initiation	Meeting with the Godhead	1. Sacred Marriage to the Goddess, or		
Initiation	Meeting with the Godhead	2. Atonement with the Father, or		
Initiation	Meeting with the Godhead	3. Apotheosis		
Initiation	The Ultimate Boon—the Elixir of Life Received			
Return	Return to the Ordinary World with the Elixir			
Return	Master of Two Worlds—Heaven and Earth			

Advanced Work

12. Using your study story, compare the story timing (chapter ten) with the timing of the mythological milestones.
13. For the story you are writing, compare the timing of your story with possible mythological milestones. Analyze whether or not you are trying to force one into the other.

Chapter Eleven: Literary Salon

1. Is Campbell's theory still relevant today?
2. Should it be changed? If so, how might it be further developed to reflect today's struggles, values, and ideology?
3. Choose a real-life issue from the recent past that has been resolved. How might the events fit into the milestones of the hero's journey?

NOTES:

Chapter Twelve
A Moment in Heaven with Aldous Huxley

Chapter Twelve explores the most esoteric aspect of writing by defying all logic to cross the threshold of mystery.

We follow Aldous Huxley's journey searching for a universal understanding of the spiritual realm. His quest was to find similarity among the differing sacred texts of the world. Huxley found 27 points of similarity—the universal understanding of the godhead.

Stories that convey one of these points resonate deeply in the human unconscious. They are what imbues great art with greatness.

Chapter Twelve Individual Exercises

1. What is the moral or spiritual message of your story?
2. The table below lists the Universal Grammar of Story™ interpretation and simplification of twelve of Aldous Huxley's points of the Perennial Philosophy. Does one of these describe the spiritual underpinning, or moral of your story? If so, how does it appear in your story?

Table 4: Universal Grammar of Story™ Interpretation of Huxley

Simplified Theme	Meaning
The Divine Is Everywhere	The Divine can be found wherever we are. We need not journey to a special place to experience the presence
The Divine Cannot Be Described	Language is too limited to convey the immense nature of the Divine
All Saints Have the Same Personality	The saints are one in purity, kindness, forgiveness, androgyny, etc.
Good Deeds Do Not Bring Salvation	Performing good deeds does not void our sins

Destruction Follows Arrogance	Those with excessive egos always crash and burn
Creativity Yields Both Good and Bad	Everything exists in balance. When we make something good, a shadow side inevitably emerges. There is no true win-win
Self-Punishment Is Easier than Ego Release	It's easier to beat yourself up than to humble yourself
Power Knows No Restraint	The more power we have, the more we pursue
Cleverness Becomes the Enemy	When we fix our eyes on cleverness, we blind ourselves to divine greatness
Three Faces of Grace	Peace comes when we live in accord with our physical body, our relationships with others, and relationship with the Divine
Evil Is Anything Not Moving Toward God	The pursuit of anything other than genuine humility creates misery
None May Suffer in Place of Another	You can't prevent others from the suffering they need to experience in order to evolve

3. What elements grant your story a sense of mystery or spiritual experience?
4. The following table lists all 27 of Huxley's original themes. Do any of these resonate with your story? If so, how?

Table 5: Huxley's Original Themes

Huxley's Original Themes
That Art Thou
The Nature of the Ground
Personality, Sanctity, Divine Incarnation
God in the World
Charity
Mortification, Non-Attachment, Right Livelihood
Truth
Religion and Temperament
Self-Knowledge
Grace and Free Will

Good and Evil
Time and Eternity
Salvation, Deliverance, Enlightenment
Immortality and Survival
Silence
Prayer
Suffering
Faith
God is not mocked
Tantum religio potuit suadere malorum (religion can persuade to evil).
Idolatry
Emotionalism
The Miraculous
Ritual, Symbol, Sacrament
Spiritual Exercises
Perseverance and Regularity
Contemplation, Action, and Social Utility

5. Table 6 lists the Seven Deadly Sins. Do any of these fit your story?

Table 6: The Seven Deadly Sins

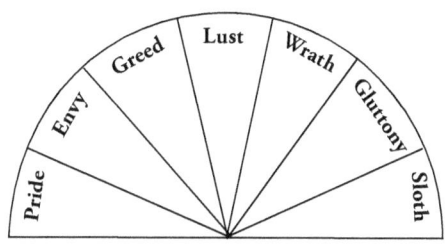

Chapter Twelve Literary Salon

1. Discuss which point in the two tables above best describes the spiritual philosophy of the salon study story.
2. Discuss which one might work in each member's story.

3. Discuss which one seems most common in contemporary stories. Are there other points beyond Huxley's 27 that might be added to the list? If so, what might they be?

Figure 1: Universal Grammar of Story™ Chart of Theories

Huxley's Perennial Philosophy	Polti's 36 Situations	The Universal Grammar of Story				Campbell's Mythology
				Timing		
					Film Timing	
		The Proposition	1. The hero's inner conflict.	Introduction		
			2. The Unity of Opposites.		First 10%	min/pp. 1-12
		State of Affairs	3. The destabilizing situation.			Call to adventure
			4. The stakes.		Second 10%	min/pp 12-24
			5. The potential resolution to the conflict			Refusal of the call
		The Challenge & The Dramatic Question		The Point of No Return	20%	min/p. 25
				The Doldrums	33%	min/p. 40
				Midpoint Reversal of Fortunes	50%	min/p. 55
				All Hope is Lost		
				Defeat of the Ego		
		The Climax			66%	min/p. 85
						Meeting with the Godhead
						1. Sacred marriage
						2. Atonement with the Father, or
						3. Apotheosis
		The Miracle				min/p. 86
						The Ultimate Boon - the Elixir of Life Received
		The Resolution			Remaining 33%	min/pp 88-115/118
						Crossing the return threshold
						Return to the ordinary world with the elixir
						Master of two worlds

Huxley: *Mystical Philosophy/The Moral*
Polti: *The Plot Situation*
Campbell (Departure from the Known World and Initiation): Crossing the first threshold, Supernatural aid, The Belly of the Whale, Road of Trials
Campbell phases: Initiation; Return

EXAMPLE ANSWERS

(There are no Example Answers for Chapters 3, 5, 6 and 7 where exercises are self explanatory.)

NOTES:

Example Answers: Prerequisites Exercises

Example Answers
1. Type of Work: Stage play in three acts. Working Title: *Bite Your Tongue*.
2. Comedy or Tragedy: A comedy. Although it has serious elements, it is more of a comedy.
3. Genres and Meanings: At first, I thought *Bite Your Tongue* was a satire. But I changed my mind when I realized that a satire has consistent biting comedy from beginning to end. *Bite Your Tongue* has elements of satire, but not consistently so. It's funny yet underlying the comedy is a heartbreaking family drama. That makes it a tragicomedy. It's not a comedy-drama because while it is a mix of comedy and drama, the tragic/heartbreaking element is stronger than simple drama.

Table 7: Genres and Meanings

Genre	Meaning
Adventure	Energetic, physical adventure into the unknown
Allegorical Fable	A moral fable using allegory for hard truth (i.e. *Animal Farm*)
Animal Story	Projecting human characteristics and norms to the animal world (i.e. *Charlotte's Web*)
Bildungsroman	A coming of age story centered on moral and emotional transformation of the hero (i.e. Kipling's *Captains Courageous* or Lee Jeong-hyang's *The Way Home*)
Black comedy	Humor derived from the bad luck or bad behavior of characters
Children's Story	Stories about children for children
Comedy of manners	Mocking the ruling/upper/aristocratic class
Comedy-drama	A balance of comedy and drama but still falling under comedy as the drama is secondary to the fundamental purpose of laughter.
Crime	From the criminal point of view

Detective Story	From a detective's perspective
Dystopia	Suffering or injustice, usually from a totalitarian or post-apocalyptic government
Ecotopia	Garden of Eden world
Epistolary	A story in the form of letters, (i.e. *The Color Purple* or *The Girls of Riyad*)
Eutopia	An ideal, harmonious world
Family Drama	The dynamics focus on family survival amid upheaval, (i.e. Zeitlin's *Beasts of the Southern Wild*, or Lixin Fan's *The Last Train Home*)
Fantasy	Imaginary beings in a real or alternate world where magic and supernatural happenings are the norm
Farce	High energy comedy of unpleasant and embarrassing situations punctuated with fateful coincidences
Fictional Autobiography	A fictional person's life story as if written by that person
Fictional biography	A fictional person's life story
Folk Tale	Fairy tales or other folk fables
Gothic Tale	Mystery and horror in an isolated, pseudo-medieval setting, with strange and/or dangerous events
Horror	Scary supernatural entities creating fear and dread
Love Story	The human capacity to love under any circumstances. The love story moves past infatuation to explore how someone comes to place another first and foremost through self-sacrifice. Not to be confused with romance stories where the goal is sexual union by overcoming forbidden or unrequited love
Melodrama	Simple plots appealing to strong emotion
Mystery	An intellectually engaging story driven by curiosity
Noble Wildman	The natural person free from the imprisonment of "civilization" who brings philosophical enlightenment to "the civilized"
Parody	A humorous imitation of a serious work of literature
Pastiche	Imitating the motifs and techniques of another time period or style
Picaresque	Humorous episodic adventures of a rough and dishonest but likeable rascal
Psychological Drama	Immense emotional pressure drives the hero to madness (i.e. *Hamlet*)

EXAMPLE ANSWERS: PREREQUISTES EXERCISES • 83

Romance	The struggle to merge one's self with another. The ultimate goal is the blending of intertwining lives symbolized in sexual union
Romantic comedy	A lighthearted story of the perils and complications of love
Romp	A rowdy comedy
Satire	Mocking the sins of the ego, (i.e. arrogance, vanity and the seven deadly sins)
Science fiction	Humanity removed from nature
Slapstick or Screwball Comedy	Fast action with ridiculous situations and physical humor
Swashbuckler	An adventure story in which the hero accomplishes great feats to aid a noble cause
Thriller	Built around triggering fear and dread in the hero and audience
Tragedy	A struggle ending in catastrophe
Tragicomedy	Funny and yet heartbreaking. Falls under comedy
Travelogue	Travel story, (i.e. *Rabbit-Proof Fence, Smoke Signals*)
Vive la résistance!	The oppressed rise up
Wilderness Story	Nature as transformative force

4. Character Types: The protagonist of *Bite Your Tongue* is Mr. Saturn. The character types describing him are: Commander, Bossy One, Enforcer, Father Figure (strict authority for the greater good), and School Principal. He's a bit of a loner or the "lonely man at the top."

Table 8: Character Types

Beloved Outlaw	Ferryman, guide over impossible obstacles	Mentor
A Chosen One	Foreigner	Monster
Adolescent, recalcitrant	Genius, Absent-Minded	Mother nourishing, loving
Big Guy, Boisterous friendly fun	Genius, Criminal	Muscleman/ Strongman/Bouncer
Big Guy, intimidating, strongman, bouncer	Genius, Mad Scientist	Nerd

Bland Nice Guy	Gentle Giant, intimidating good hearted	Noble Knight
Blind Seer	God or Goddess, all powerful with human qualities	Noble Wildman, free of "civilizations" rules
Bossy One	Good King	Outlaw
Caregiver	Grande Dame	Peacemaker
Champion	Grotesque physical form, misunderstood but with a heart of gold	Pessimist
Childlike, loves adventure, simplicity	Harlequin /Jester	Philosopher/Sage
Commander	Herald	Pixie Girl, high energy. eccentric, cute
Conscience	Hero, intent on saving the day	Priest, who displays his whiskey /cigarettes
Contender underdog	Hotshot skilled, but reckless.	Psychopath
Corrupter, illuminates everyone's dark side	Hunter of Monsters	Rebel
Creative One	Imposter/Pretender	School Master/ Principal
Disciplinarian	Ingenue	Seductress/Seducer
Egomaniac	Initiator	Seeker
Elder, enduring	Innocent Monster doesn't realize they are a monster	Shrew, a bad-tempered/aggressive woman
Elder, grumpy	Innocent, sweet one next door	Socially Challenged
Elder, wise	Jock not so smart athlete	Storyteller
Elderly Master	Joe America, athletic or healthy Mr. Nice Guy	Swashbuckler, joyful, noisy, and boastful renaissance era swordsman or pirate
Enforcer	Loner	Teacher

Evil fighter	Loser	Thief, sophisticated/socialite
Evil Lord	Lovable Rogue	Tomboy
Explorer	Loveable Rogue	Tortured Artist
Facilitator	Loyalist	Town Drunk
Fall Guy, The scapegoat	Magician	Traveler
Farm Boy	Magician or Shaman	Trickster
Father Figure, authority with loving heart.	Mamma's Boy	Village Idiot
Father Figure, strict authority for the greater good	Maverick	Wise Fool
Femme Fatale (traitorous)	Mentally Challenged	Wise Old Man

5. Symbolic Family Role: Mr. Saturn is the archetypal uncle in charge. The sentiment is of his having taken responsibility for the children from weaker siblings. In his uncle-come-father-figure role he feels somewhat distant from his charges making his strict authority for the greater good seem colder than it would for a father.

The following table lists archetypal roles in an extended/tribal family and how these roles are shaped by the way individuals come into their family.

Table 9: Archetypal Family Roles

Role	Full-blooded from both parents	Half-blooded from one parent	Step-member, child brought in through marriage	Chosen member, brought in through adoption	In-law, adult brought in through marriage	Ghost or memory of a lost one
Parent						
Father						
Mother						
Child						
Daughter						
Son						
Sibling						
Sister						
Brother						
Grandparent						
Paternal Grandfather						
Maternal Grandfather						
Paternal Grandmother						
Maternal Grandmother						
Parental Sibling						
Paternal Uncle						
Maternal Uncle						
Paternal Aunt						
Maternal Aunt						
Grandchild						
Grandson						
Granddaughter						
Cousin						
Cousin Male						
Cousin Female						

6. Protagonist's Name: Jason Saturn. He goes by Mr. Saturn. Saturn means the restricting, controlling, limiting father figure. Jason means the healer. In the story of Jason and the Argonauts, this name alludes to the work of Chiron, the wounded healer. Mr. Saturn is trying to heal the world's woes but he himself is wounded and trying to work from limiting position.

7. Protagonists Social Function: Mr. Saturn is the opinion giver, critic, and manager.

The table below offers a list of common social functions.

Table 10: Social Functions for Characters

Role	Meaning
Aggressor	The bully who thrives on attacking the value and work of the group or its individuals
Blocker	Unreasonably negative, resistant, and disagreeable
Good Mother/ Cheerleader	Encourages everyone with understanding, acceptance and praise to encourage progress through warmth and cohesion
Clarifier	Elaborates on the ideas and processes to predict the final outcome based on the strategies and resources at hand. Analytical not visionary
Complainer	Focuses on what is unpleasant, unsatisfying, and needs to change.
Compromiser	Willing to set some personal desires aside for the group
Coordinator	The one arranging the group to work best
Demanding absolute answers	Highly uncomfortable with ambiguity. Needs a "written in stone" approach
Dominator	A leader figure focused on commanding authority over others through positive or negative means. Differs from the bully who attacks for the sheer feeling of power.
Doubting Thomas	The skeptic who demands clear evidence
Energizer	A father figure who stimulates the group to a higher quality of process and outcome
Gossip	Spreads scandalous or false information for dramatic effect
Gatekeeper	Facilitates the flow of communication for everyone's participation, keeps fruitful channels open and problem channels closed
Group Observer	The diarist who interprets group ideas and behaviors for a global understanding of issues
Harmonizer	Reconciles differences between members generating conflict. Brings relief through humor and a peaceful/delightful presence

Help Seeker	Unreasonably seeks sympathy from the group for inappropriate/personal issues
Homesteader	Refuses to budge on their position or opinion regardless of overwhelming evidence that it is unhelpful or unwise
Quiet One	Shy group member who is reluctant or unable to articulate their ideas.
Information giver	Offer authoritative facts from credible sources for group use
Information seeker	Looking to clarify facts and substantiate them with authoritative information
Initiator	Offers new ideas and novel perspective for problem solving
Joker	Bored child figure uninvolved with the group, distracts with horseplay
Monopolizer	Attention seeker believing their opinion is more important than others
Opinion Giver	Talks excessively preventing others from participating
Opinion Seeker	Clarifies values about group effort and goals from members
Optimizer	Seeks group efficiency
Peacemaker	Seeking harmony by getting opposing sides to see each other's perspectives
Procedural Technician	Keeping the rules of order in play
Questioner	Often seeks trivial or unnecessary information
Rambler	Unfocused, digressing into unrelated subjects with confusing language
Reality Tester	Tests group accomplishment
Recognition Seeker	Call attention to themselves for personal validation
Recorder	The group secretary and/or diarist
Self-Confessor	Inappropriately offers an uncomfortable amount of self-disclosure
Summarizer	Creates/Affirms group consensus at close of topic discussion and/or events
Supporter	Mother figure assuaging insecurities and boosting confidence
Critic	Quality control person focusing on lacking or incorrect elements
Manager	The self-appointed group leader

8. Profession: Mr. Saturn is a high school principal at a rural public boarding school.

The table below offers a list of professions.

Table 11: Professions for Characters

Anthropologist	Driver, Dump Truck	Mechanic	Scientist, Mathematician
Accountant	Driver, Taxi	Mechanic, Heavy Machinery	Scientist, Medical Researcher
Actor	Driver, Train	Medical Assistant	Scientist, Physics
Acupuncturist	Drug Dealer	Medical Lab Technician	Scribe
Administrative Assistant	Drywaller	Menu Planner	Secretary
Administrative Manager	Elected Executive (Governor, Mayor)	Merchant	Senior Official
Administrative Specialized Secretaries	Elected Official, Low Level	Middleman Logistics	Set Designer
Advertising Executive	Electrician	Midwife	Shepard
Agricultural Production Manager	Emergency Dispatcher	Military Non-commissioned	Sheriff
Agricultural Worker, Skilled	Engineer	Military Officer	Ship Captain
Agricultural Worker, Unskilled	Engineering Professionals	Milkman	Ship Crew
Animal Producer	Entertainer	Mime	Ship's cook
Architect	Factory worker	Miner	Shoemaker
Archivist	Farmer	Mining Company Manager	Shop Clerk

Art Installation Designer/Manager	Fast Food Worker	Mining, Tunneling	Shopkeeper
Artisan	Ferrier	Money Collector	Smith
Artist	Finish Carpenter	Museum Director	Social Worker
Assembler	Firefighter	Musician	Software Designer
Assembly Line Worker	First Mate	Naturopath	Software Technician
Astrologer	Fisheries Production Manager	Navigator	Soldier
Baker	Fisherman	Network Manager	Sports and Fitness Workers
Bank Teller	Flight Crew	Nurse	Spy, government
Banker	Food Processing Worker	Nurse - Medical Follower	Spy, industrial
Barber	Forest Firefighter	Office Workers: Place of Worship	Statisticians
Black Market Vendor	Forestry Production Manager	Operator, Car Wash	Stewardess
Bookkeeper	Gambler	Operator, Food Machine	Street Fight Manager
Border Guard	Garment Worker	Operator, Heavy Machinery	Street Sweeper
Building Maintenance	Government Regulator	Operator, Paper Product Machine	Street Vendor
Building Supervisor	Grade School Teacher	Operator, Textile	Subsistence Farmer
Business Manager	Guard	Other Service Manager	Subsistence Fisherman
Camera Operator, TV, Film	Hairdresser/Beautician	Painter, Artist	Subsistence Trash Gatherer
Captain	Handicraft Maker	Painter, Construction	Surgeon
Career Soldier	Herbalist	Papermaker	Surveyor

Champion athlete	High School Principal	Para scientist	Tailor
Champion of the underdog	Hospice Worker	Paralegal	Tax collector
Cheese Maker	Hotel Desk Clerk	Peasant	Teacher
Chef	Hotel Maid	Pharmacist	Teacher's Aid
Chief Executive	Hotel Manager	Phlebotomist	Technician, Life Sciences
Childcare Worker	Housekeeper	Photographer	Technician, Physics
Chiropractor	Hunter	Physical Therapist	Telegraph Operator
City Recorder	Husbandman	Pilot	Telephone Lineman
Cleaners/Helpers	Imam	Pimp	Telephone Operator
Cleric	Industrialist	Planner	Theater House Manager
Clerical Worker	Information Technology Service Manager	Plumber	Tinker
Clerk, Boutique	Ingenue	Police	Toolmaker
Comedian	inspector	Police Dispatcher	Trader
Communications Technology Manager	Inventory Clerk	Priest/Minister	Translator
Con Man, Business	Jailer	Principal/School Master	Trapper
Con Man, Entertainment	Janitor	Professional Services Manager	Trash Collector
Con Man, Religious	Journalist	Professor	Travel Agency Clerk
Confessor/ Psychologist	Journalist, Radio	Prostitute	Travel Agent
Construction Laborer	Judge	Protective Service Worker	Undertaker
Cook	Keyboard Data Input	Psychiatrist	Vendor, Flea Market

Coroner	Kitchen worker	Public Relations	Veterinarian
Court Reporter	Laborer, Farm	Purchasing Agent	Vineyard Owner
Cowboy	Laborer, Fish Processing	Quality Control	Vocational Instructor
Curator	Laborer, Forest	Rabbi	Waiter/Waitress
Dairyman	Lawyer	Radio Arts/ Culture Show	Warrior/ Commander
Dancer	Leather Products Maker	Radio Show Host	Warrior/Soldier
Database Manager	Legal Secretary	Refuse Workers	Washer woman
Delivery Driver, Bicycle	Librarian	Reporter	Wedding Planner
Delivery Driver, Motorcycle	Livestock Farmer	Restaurant Manager	Welder
Delivery Driver, Van/Truck	Locksmith	Restaurateur	Wholesale Trade Manager
Designer, Fashion	Logger	Retail Store Manager	Window Washer
Detective/ Investigator	Machinery Repairman	Sailor	Wine Maker
Director, Film	Machinist	Sales Manager	Witch
Director, Theatre	Managing Director	Salesman	Writer
Disability Assistant	Marketing Manager	Scientist	X-Ray Technician
Doctor	Masseuse	Scientist, Astronomy	Yogi
Dog Fight/Cock Fight Promoter/ Manager	Master of Ceremonies	Scientist, Biologist	
Driver	Mathematician	Scientist, Earth	

9. Disposition: Mr. Saturn is serious, practical, realistic, forceful, moral, rigid, self-assured, self-reliant, conservative, and controlling.

The table below offers a sample list of character dispositions.

Table 12: Character Dispositions

Abstract	Cruel	Impatient	Placid	Severe
Action Oriented	Curious	Impractical	Playful	Shameless
Adaptable	Defiant	Impulsive	Polite	Shrewd
Adventurer	Delicate	Independent	Practical	Shy
Aesthetic	Dependent	Indifferent	Pragmatist	Sloppy
Aggressive	Diplomatic	Insecure	Pretentious	Slow
Aloof	Disrespectful	Intellectual	Private	Social
Altruistic	Dominate	Interdependent	Proper	Socialite
Analytical	Dreamer	Introvert	Prudent	Socializer
Anxious	Dreamy	Intuitive	Quiet	Solitary
Apathetic	Earthy	Inventive	Quitter	Spiritual
Apprehensive	Easy-Going	Irresponsible	Radical	Spontaneous
Attentive	Eccentric	Jealous	Rational	Stability Valuing
Bold	Egotistical	Joyful	Reactive	Structure
Bombastic	Emotional	Kind	Realist	Suspicious

Calculating	Emotionally Stable	Laissez-faire	Reasonable	Sympathetic
Calm	Energetic	Liberal	Rebel	Taciturn
Carefree	Expedient	Lively	Refined	Tender
Careful	Experimental	Loner	Relaxed	Tense
Careless	Extrovert	Lower Consciousness	Reserved	Theoretical
Cautious	Faith	Lower Intellect	Respectful	Thoughtful
Challenging	Fanatic	Loyal	Responsible	Timid
Chance	Foolish	Materialistic	Restrained	Tough
Change Valuing	Forceful	Melancholy	Rigid	Traditional
Chaotic	Forthright	Merciful	Rough	Tranquil
Cheerful	Friendly	Modest	Rude	Treasonus
Cold/Distant	Genuine	Moral	Rule-Conscious	Trusting
Communal	Grounded	Narcissistic	Rule-follower	Unabashed
Compassionate	Guilt-Free	Need to Influence	Ruthless	Uncaring
Concrete	Guilt-Prone	Nervous	Secure	Unconcerned with thoughts of others
Confident	haphazardly or disorderly	Neurotic	Self-Assured	Unconscientious

Conforming	Hardened	Non-conforming	Self-Blaming	Uncontrollable
Conscientious	Harsh	Obedient	Self-Control	Undisciplined
Conservative	Hedonistic	Obstructive	Self-Critical	Unemotional
Consistent	Hermit	Open	Self-Indulgent	Uninhibited
Content	Hesitant	Organized	Self-Reliant	Unpretentious
Controlled	Higher Consciousness	Outgoing	Self-restrained	Unreasonable
Controlling	Higher Intellect	Over Wrought	Self-Righteous	Unruffled
Conventional	Homebody	Pacifist	Self-sacrificing	Unsentimental
Cooperative	Humble	Paranoid	Self-Satisfied	Utilitarian
Corrupt	Hypocritical	Patient	Sensible	Vicious
Courageous	Hysterical	Perfectionist	Sensitive	Vigilant
Coward	Idealistic	Persistent	Sentimental	Warm
Critical	Imaginative	Philosophical	Serious	Warm Friendly

10. Sparking the Plot
    A. The opposite of commander is maverick.
    B. The opposite of serious-realistic is playful-dreamer.
    C. The force that the serious, realistic and commanding Mr. Saturn will encounter comes in the form of a playful dreaming maverick.
11. Brief Description of the Story
    A. Gathering the answers from 1-10:

1) Bite Your Tongue, a stage play in three acts.
2) Comedy.
3) Tragicomedy.
4) Commander, the Father Figure, strict authority for the greater good.
5) Mr. Saturn's archetypal family role is the birth paternal uncle in charge. The sentiment is of his having taken responsibility for the children from weaker siblings.
6) Mr. Saturn, meaning a restricting, controlling, limiting father figure. Jason meaning wounded healer.
7) Group coordinator and the critic.
8) High school principal.
9) Realist, forceful, moral, rigid, self-assured, self-reliant, conservative, and controlling.
10) The force the hero encounters is a playful dreamer in the form of a maverick.

B. Brief summary of the story: *Bite Your Tongue* is a comedy play in three acts about a strict, commanding principal whose quiet world is turned upside down by a loud, playfully dreaming, lovable rogue who brings chaos and scandal to a rural public boarding high school in the isolated cowboy west.

Example Answers: Chapter One

Story Description Exercises:

1. Mind map for *The Miracle Worker*

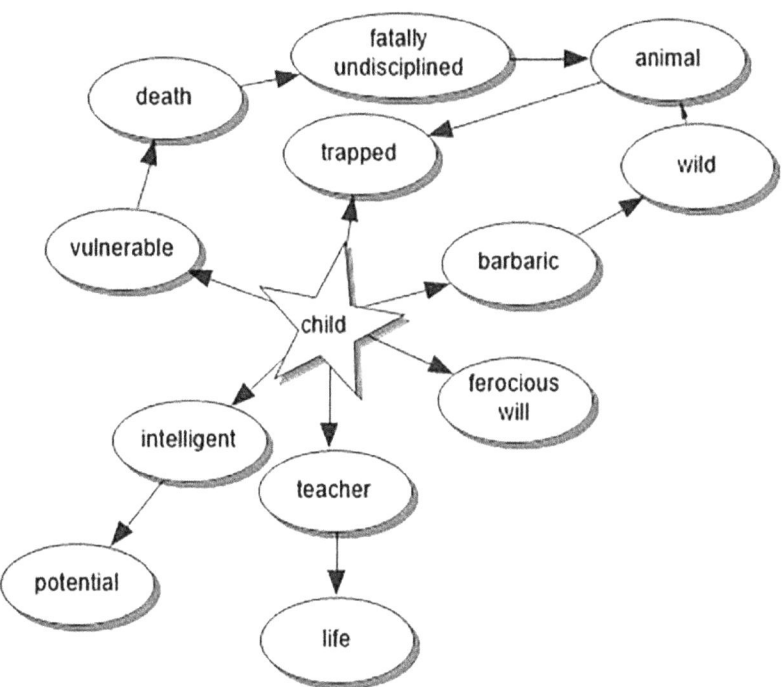

Figure 2: Mind Map for The Miracle Worker

2. For the study story *The Miracle Worker*: An intelligent child is trapped inside her own barbaric and ferociously fatal will. (To keep this very general, not even the disability is mentioned).

3. Simple description of *The Miracle Worker*: an intelligent but violently undisciplined, animal-like child faces death from her own ferocious will unless she yields to the fierce discipline of an iron-willed teacher intent on breaking past the child's defiance to reach the intelligent being within.

4. I was attracted to this study story because I easily identified with Helen as an ignorant person yearning for knowledge but trapped within a ferocious will. Ironically, I was my own iron-willed teacher intent on breaking past my own defiance. Through both characters I saw myself struggling to awaken to intellectual enlightenment.
5. Repeating #1: In my story *Bite Your Tongue* the mind-map looks like this:

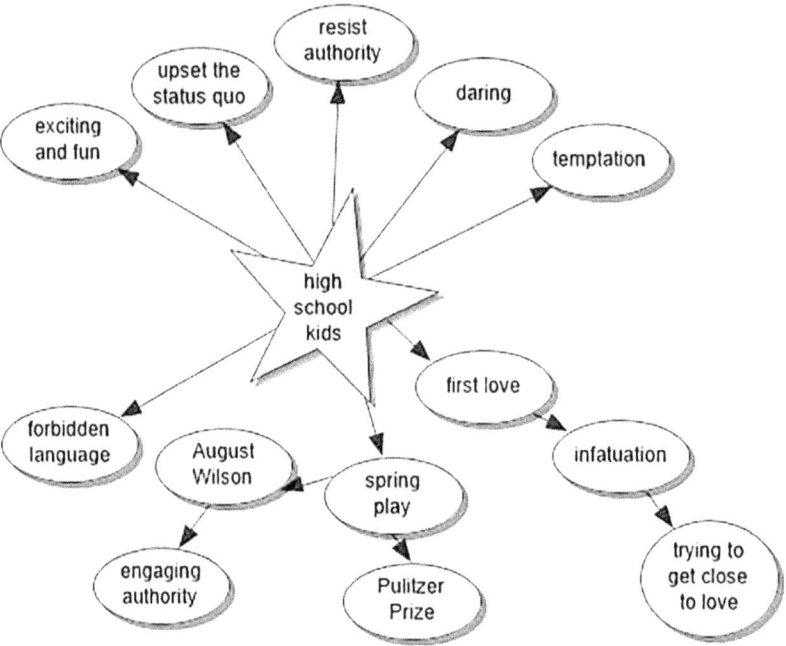

Figure 3: Mind Map for Bite Your Tongue

Repeating #2: The characters in *Bite Your Tongue* depict the tension of the young naturally resisting authority by upsetting the status quo. Here, they use another status quo to do it. This is the story about a group of adolescents wanting to enact a beloved story written in a language forbidden to them. Yet that story has won the highest prize in the land which ironically centers it firmly in the status quo.

Repeating #3: Now I'm looking for a simple description, general enough to apply to any story, anywhere, at any time in history: These adolescents upset the status quo (mandating only standard language be spoken in school) by engaging another status quo (great literary plays should be performed). In this case, the great play was written in nonstandard language. The metaphor could be one of revealing hypocrisy, but it also might be one of embracing something beloved but forbidden.

Repeating #4: I was attracted to *Bite Your Tongue* as a means of exposing the hypocrisy of my family's valuing education for some members but not for me. I wanted to explore, reveal, and share my beloved intellect but was forbidden.

Character Relationship Exercises A-F:

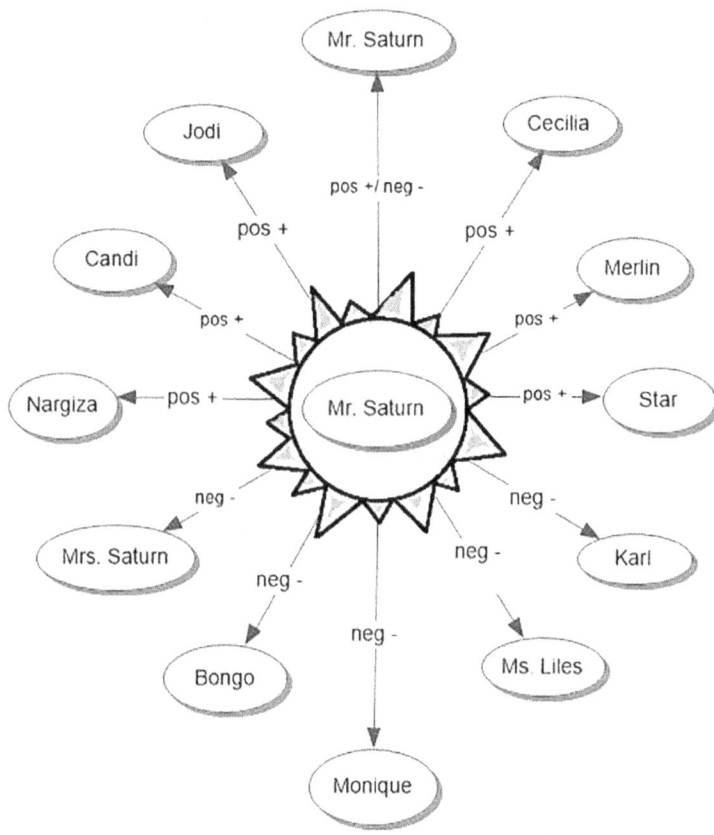

Figure 4: Positive/Negative Character Relationships for Bite Your Tongue

Exercise 12A.

> **To Mr. Saturn**
> Monique represents everything that is wrong with the world.
> Jodi represents a child to be saved.
> Bongo represents a child who can't be saved.
> Ms. Liles represents clay to be shaped.
> Star represents everything that is right in the world
> Karl represents arrogance to be disciplined.
> Nargiza represents the ideal American.
> Cecilia represents the purity of the world.
> Candi represents the unpleasantries we're

Exercise 12B. (For one other character)

> **To Monique**
> Mr. Saturn represents a child to save.
> Jodi represents Clay to be shaped.
> Bongo represents the purity of the world.
> Ms. Liles represents clay to be shaped.
> Star represents cynical reality.
> Karl represents everything that is wrong with the world.
> Nargiza represents the ideal American.
> Candi represents human endurance.
> Cecilia represents the oppressed class.
> Mrs. Saturn represents the reason children need saving.

Example Answers: Chapter Two

1. *The Miracle Worker* is a story solidly from modernity with its emphasis on institutional logic and scientific advancement over tribal reunion. The elements representing this are the scientific writings providing the authority undergirding Anne's approach, which would be disregarded without it. For a postmodern audience the story would need to reconcile Jimmy's alienation from the family, see how Anne comes into the fold, and have better development of Viney and her children. Percy and Martha provide the role model for normal children but remain outsiders within the story. A postmodern story would show Kate envious of Viney's mother/children interaction.
2. In *Bite Your Tongue* the craving for reconnection is central to the movement of the story. In every scene, we see Mr. Saturn lamenting the scattering of his own family and fiercely trying to keep his students together by protecting them from the outside world.
3. Generational Primal Archetypes table for *The Miracle Worker*:

Table 13: Example of Generational Primal Archetypes for The Miracle Worker

Story Title: *The Miracle Worker*		Author: William Gibson
Archetype	**Function**	**Character**
Father	Leader, imposer of order, the status quo	Captain Keller, Anne
Mother	Nurturer, comforter, intercessor of the father	Kate
Child	Innocent, vulnerable figure, eager for exploration.	Percy, Martha, Aunt Ev, to some degree Viney
God	All powerful creator. The purely good one of whom all are in awe	In the end it is Anne

Devil	The self-focused seemingly arrogant one	Anne, Helen, James
Wise Grandfather	Guru, intercessor of God, masterful transformer of Devil	Anne's books, Anagnos
Wise Grandmother	Crone, nurturing magic maker, balancing creation & destruction	Anne, to some degree Viney
Trickster	Resister of the status quo	Helen, James, Anne
Archetypal Hero	The everyday person at the highest level of virtue	Anne
Archetypal Villain	The character blocking the hero's movement.	Helen

Example Answers: Chapter Four

1. For an example of bad logic using the logical syllogism, I analyzed the reasoning a friend of mine used to maintain a severe addiction to sugary soda and continue drinking several liters of it every day.

Table 14: Example of Bad Logical Reasoning

Major premise	Sugary soda is bad when it causes diabetes.
Minor Premise	Sugary soda does not cause me diabetes.
Conclusion	Therefore, sugary soda is not bad for me.

My friend was right that sugar did not cause him diabetes. In fact, he still does not have diabetes even after the liver transplant he needed from the sugar indulgence leading him to develop nonalcoholic steatohepatitis causing complete liver failure. What he missed with his major premise was that excessive sugar consumption can cause many different kinds of serious health problems, not just diabetes.

The correct syllogism for my friend (which he now adheres to) is:

Table 15: Example of Corrected Logical Reasoning

Major premise	Excessive sugar is bad for human health
Minor Premise	I am a human
Conclusion	Therefore, excessive sugar is bad for my health.

Example Answers: Chapter Eight

Example Answers Eight: Unity of Opposite Pairs

Table 16: Examples of Unity of Opposite Pairs

Adaptable/Rigid	Hedonistic/Self-Controlled	Quitter/Persistent
Adventurer/Homebody	Hermit/Socialite	Radical/Apathetic
Anxious/Unruffled	Higher Consciousness/Lower Consciousness	Rational/Intuitive
Attentive/Aloof	Hypocritical/Genuine	Realistic/Idealistic
Blunt/Refined	Hysterical/Unemotional	Reasonable/Unreasonable
Bold/Timid	Imaginative/Analytical	Rebel/Proper
Bombastic/Refined	Impulsive/Restrained	Relaxed/Tense
Carefree/Self-Restrained	Independent/Dependent	Reserved/Warm
Careful/Careless	Independent/Interdependent	Respectful/Disrespectful
Compassionate/cruel	Insecure/Secure	Responsible/Irresponsible
Concrete/Abstract	Inventive/Consistent	Rough/Refined
Concrete/Theoretical	Jealous/Content	Rule-Follower/Laissez-Faire
Conforming/Nonconforming	Kind/Vicious	Self-Assured/Apprehensive
Conscientious/Unconscientious	Liberal/Conservative	Self-Critical/Self-Assured
Conservative/Liberal	Lively/Placid	Self-Indulgent/Self-Sacrificing
Controlled/Chaotic	Loner/Communal	Self-Reliant/Dependent

Controlled/Undisciplined	Loner/Socializer	Self-Righteous/Humble
Controlling/Uncontrollable	Lower Intellect/Higher Intellect	Self-Satisfied/Self-Blaming
Cooperative/Obstructive	Loyal/Treasonous	Sensitive/Harsh
Coward/Courageous	Materialistic/Spiritual	Sentimental/Unsentimental
Curious/Cautious	Melancholy/Joyful	Serious/Lively
Defiant/Obedient	Merciful/Ruthless	Severe/Playful
Dominate/Independent	Modest/Shameless	Shy/Unabashed
Dreamer/Pragmatist	Moral/Corrupt	Slow/Energetic
Easy-Going/Critical	Narcissistic/Altruistic	Social/Solitary
Eccentric/Conventional	Need to Influence others/Unconcerned with thoughts of others	Spiritual/Rational
Egotistical/Humble	Nervous/Confident	Spontaneous/Calculating
Emotional/Rational	Neurotic/Calm	Stability Valuing/Change Valuing
Emotionally Stable/Reactive	Open/Private	Structure/Chance
Energetic/Quiet	Organized/Sloppy+A81	Suspicious/Trusting
Expedient/Rule-Conscious	Outgoing/Reserved	Sympathetic/Uncaring
Extrovert/Introvert	Pacifist/Aggressive	Taciturn/Cheerful
Faith/Action	Paranoid/Sensible	Thoughtful/Foolish
Fanatic/Indifferent	Patient/Impatient	Timid/Forceful
Forthright/Diplomatic	Perfectionist/Expedient	Tough/Delicate
Friendly/Challenging	Perfectionist/Haphazardly or Disorderly	Traditional/Experimental
Genuine/Shrewd	Philosophical/Practical	Tranquil/Over Wrought

Grounded/Dreamy	Polite/Rude	Trusting/Vigilant
Guilt-Free/Guilt-Prone	Practical/Impractical	Unpretentious/Pretentious
Hardened/Tender	Private/Open	Utilitarian/Aesthetic
Commander/Maverick	Prudent/Spontaneous	Warm Hearted /Cold Distant
Strict/ Rebellious	Authoritative/Humanistic	Stern/Mirthful
Stern/Charismatic	Commanding/Freewheeling	

Exercise #10, Hero Villain Polarity

Table 17: Hero Villain Polarity Example

Title: *Bite Your Tongue*   by *Hazel Denhart*

Hero---Antihero
Commanding   *Maverick*
Defining Adjective   Defining Adjective

Characteristic Traits of the Hero: *Stern, commanding, serious, disciplined, cold, distant.*

Characteristic Traits of the antihero: *Playful, maverick, funny, spontaneous, warm, loving.*

Characteristics they have in common: *commitment to education, dedication to students.*

Choose a single adjective to identify the commonality between the two: *Dedicated.*

Mark the point where the adjective of commonality falls on the continuum of polarity. Does it fall balanced in the center? Or is it more toward the side of one character or the other?

Adjective of Commonality
Dedicated

Hero-----------------------------XXXX---------------------------Antihero
Commanding   *Playful*
Defining Adjective   Defining Adjective

Exercise #12, Polar Movement

The table below offers an example of steps for the incremental movement from insensitivity to compassion using a modified version of Egri's work.

Table 18: Example of Incremental Polar Movement

From Insensitive to Compassionate
1. Self-centered protection from old emotional injury
2. Causing injury to another through thoughtlessness
3. Justifying the injury as a teaching moment
4. Having doubts about the injury
5. Reevaluation of the injury
6. Remorse
7. Humility
8. False generosity to the injured
9. Feeling unsatisfied with the generosity
10. Reevaluation
11. Discovery of the other's point of view
12. Humility
13. Authentic compassion
14. Real generosity rooted in sacrifice

Example Answers: Chapter Nine

Exercise # 1: Sample Answer

Table 19: Example of The Five Elements of the Hero's Proposition for *The Miracle Worker*

The Five Elements of the Hero's Proposition	
Title: *The Miracle Worker* **Author: William Gibson**	
A. Hero's Inner Conflict	*An inner weakness or vulnerability in tension with an opposing need that causes the hero constant trouble in life*
	For Helen, the inner weakness is her undisciplined tyranny. The opposing need is a desperate need for human communication. Her need to communicate is sabotaged by her own tyranny
B. Unity of Opposites	*A single adjective describing the hero and its antonym for the antihero*
	Undisciplined/Disciplined
C. Destabilizing Situation	*A deteriorating situation triggering a psychological journey forcing the hero to confront and overcome the inner weakness*
	Anne's arrival brings serious challenge to Helen's tyrannical rule
D. The Stakes	*The risk of losing something of life and death importance to the hero*
	Helen risks losing absolute command of her world, the only world she knows. Unbeknownst to her, she will also die in an institution if she cannot learn to communicate
E. Potential Resolution to the Conflict	*An idea appearing in the introduction to the story that hints at a way to solve the dilemma*
	Helen can turn her iron will of tyranny toward learning how to communicate

Exercise #3: The antihero blocks the hero's strengths and threaten the vulnerability in *The Miracle Worker* where Anne dismantles Helen's tyranny leaving the only path forward through her surrender to and acceptance of Anne's discipline.

Exercise #4: State of Affairs for *The Miracle Worker*

Table 20: State of Affairs for The Miracle Worker

Helen, an intelligent but brutally ignorant, strong-willed, undisciplined and
Hero   [--------------Unity of Opposites for Hero----------------------------]

badly spoiled, deaf-blind child, who desperately wants to communicate,
            [---------------------- Inner Conflict/vulnerability---------------]

and who will die if she cannot learn to, becomes the student of Anne,
         [---------the Stakes---------]   [Destabilizing Context & Potential Resolution]

a severe disciplinarian, who is charged with teaching Helen language.
[Antihero]   [Unity of Opposites for Antihero]   [Potential Resolution-------]

Example Answers: Chapter Ten

Table 21: Timing Milestones for The Miracle Worker

Title: *The Miracle Worker*, Playscript			Author: William Gibson
Timing Milestone	Expected % of story	Actual %	Description
Beginning of the Introductory Event	1-2	1-5	The triggering event comes with Helen attacking Martha with scissors, continuing with Helen turning over the baby cradle. This leads to the introductory event: the summoning of Anne
Introduction of Hero	1	1	Helen appears in the prologue scene as a baby
Introduction/ foreshadow of Antihero.	1-5	5	Anne is foreshadowed on p. 6* with Aunt Ev hoping the school in Baltimore will send someone who can help Helen. Anne physically appears on p. 12
All Principal Characters presented	11	10	By p. 12 all the characters have been introduced
Explication of the Stakes	2 - 18	16	By p. 18 we recognize that Helen is a danger to the family but that life in an institution is an unacceptable danger to her
End of introductory sequence	18-22	24	The introductory sequence is completed on p. 27 when Helen takes Anne's suitcase upstairs to the guest room
The Point of No Return/The Challenge	20-22	28	Helen knocks out Anne's tooth on p. 32
The Doldrums	37	37	Helen tosses the key down the well on p. 40

Midpoint Reversal of Fortunes	50	50		Helen is abruptly disempowered by Anne in the dining room fight scene on p. 56
All Hope Is Lost	66	66		Helen sinks sobbing to the floor in the hunting cabin on p. 75
The Climax	67	71		On p. 80, Helen pushes Percy's hand away to get Anne to spell into her hand
The Miracle	67-68			In the film version, the miracle comes with a chick hatching in Helen's hand. In the playscript, the miracle comes on p. 81, at 72% of the story where the miracle it is symbolized in a pseudo-ethereal moment unlike any other in the play. The scene takes place late at night with five shafts of moonlight lighting the anguish and hope of five characters in solitude. One shows Helen sleeping. A second shows Anne in the rocker singing. A third shows Jimmy on the porch of the main house. A fourth shows Captain Keller at the table in the family room. The fifth shows Kate pacing in Anne's room. The focus goes to Anne who gently rocks a doll while softly singing *Hush Little Baby*. Although the other characters cannot hear her, they act as if they might, or as if they are joined in a moment of prayer for a miracle. But the true miracle for Helen comes on page 108 when she suddenly understands language
Resolution	To end			Resolved at the end with Helen understanding who Anne really is and why she has come

* These page numbers are based on Gibson's 1957 play published by Knopf, see References for exact edition.

Example Answers: Chapter Eleven

Exercise #10: Example of Hero's Journey for Helen in *The Miracle Worker*

Table 22: Hero's Journey for Helen in *The Miracle Worker*

Title: *The Miracle Worker*		Author: William Gibson	
Campbell's Hero's Journey		Action by Hero	Effect on Hero's Ego
Departure	Ordinary World	A badly spoiled tyrant	Status quo
	Call to Adventure	The first lesson of the alphabet	Defiance
	Refusal of the Call	Knocking out Anne's tooth, destroying the dining room	Reinforced defiance
	Crossing the Threshold	Helen falls onto the floor in the little house in utter despair—her first act of defeat. She is in new terrain. Supernatural aid is symbolized by an ethereal moment of prayerful hope by all the family members in the moonlight. In the film, a baby chick hatches in Helen's hand	Defeat and Despondency
	Supernatural Aid		
	Belly of the Whale -- the death of the ego		

Initiation	Road of Trials -- making certain the ego is dead		Breaking the water pitcher at her homecoming. Pumping the well to refill it	Conscious awakening, release of the ego
	Meeting with the Godhead	1. Sacred Marriage to the Goddess, or		
		2. Atonement with the Father, or	Peace with Anne	
		3. Apotheosis.		
	The Ultimate Boon - the Elixir of Life Received		Authentic joy	Complete release
Return	Return to the Ordinary World with the Elixir		Sitting on Anne's lap on the porch and spelling out "Helen Loves Teacher."	Transcendence
	Master of Two Worlds - Heaven and Earth		Helen is at peace with herself and the world	

REFERENCES

Campbell, Joseph. *The Hero with a Thousand Faces*. New York: Bolligen Foundation Inc., 1949.

Denhart, Hazel. *Bite Your Tongue*. Director, Daniel Brunnet, 45 minutes. Berlin, Germany: 12th Internationales Literaturfestival Berlin: Shakespeare & Sons Books, 2012.

Denhart, Hazel. *The Universal Grammar of Story: An Author's Guide to Writing for the Soul of the World*. Seattle: Invisible Press, 2019

Egri, Lajos. *The Art of Dramatic Writing: Its Basis in the Creative Interpretation of Human Motives*. Rev. ed. New York: Simon and Schuster, 1960.

Grebanier, Bernard. *Playwriting: How to Write for the Theatre*. New York: Harper & Row, 1961.

Huxley, Aldous. *The Perennial Philosophy*. New York: Harper, 1945.

Jung, Carl G. *The Portable Jung (Portable Library)*. Translated by R. F. C. Hull. New York: Penguin Classics, 1976. First published 1971.

Jung, Carl G., and Marie-Louise von Franz. *Man and His Symbols*. Garden City, New York: Doubleday, 1964.

Gibson, William. *The Miracle Worker: A Play for Television*. First ed. New York: Knopf, 1957.

———. *The Miracle Worker*. USA: United Artists Corp., 1962.

Fan, Lixin. *The Last Train Home*. China: Zeitgeist Films, 2009.

May, Rollo. *The Courage to Create*. First ed. New York: Norton, 1975.

Polti, Georges. *The 36 Dramatic Situations*. Cincinnati, OH: James Knapp Reeve, 1921.

Price, W.T. *The Analysis of Play Construction and Dramatic Principle*. New York: W.T. Price, Publisher, 1908.

ARTIST ACKNOWLEDGEMENT
ART SERIES ABSTRACTIONS

The drawings throughout the book are abstractions of the same tree on Mt. Hood in Oregon. This is the last tree at the timberline, perched on the edge of oblivion, before the mountain slope gives way to an utterly inhospitable landscape. The drawings, like stories, first come to us as vague, amorphous ideas, taking shape step by step as they slowly shift into being. From the first tree to the tenth tree, the artist's idea wrestles its way toward concrete reality. It also seeks to remind us that life can thrive even at the very edge of existence. This tree thrives at the edge of transcendence, the place where one way of being reaches for the other. Here is the time and place where life as we know it reaches for the heavens. Stories, too, perch on the edge of life, opening the human heart to reach for the heavens.

Celebration p. ix	Over-Engineer p. xv	Cubits p.8	Collect p. 14	Map p.18
SeeMe p. 26	Precept p. 32	Reality p. 38	Cnnect p. 46	Awaken p.52
Birth p. 60	Conscious p. 68	Misstep p. 74	All images copyrighted Rick Denhart ©2020	

Notes:

Notes:

Notes:

Notes:

Notes:

Notes:

Notes:

Notes:

www.ingramcontent.com/pod-product-compliance
Lightning Source LLC
Chambersburg PA
CBHW050324120526
44592CB00014B/2038